Mandala
Artistic Coloring Books

Copyright: Published in the United States by Janice Perrine
Published January 2017
ISBN-13: 978-1542641425
ISBN-10: 154264142X

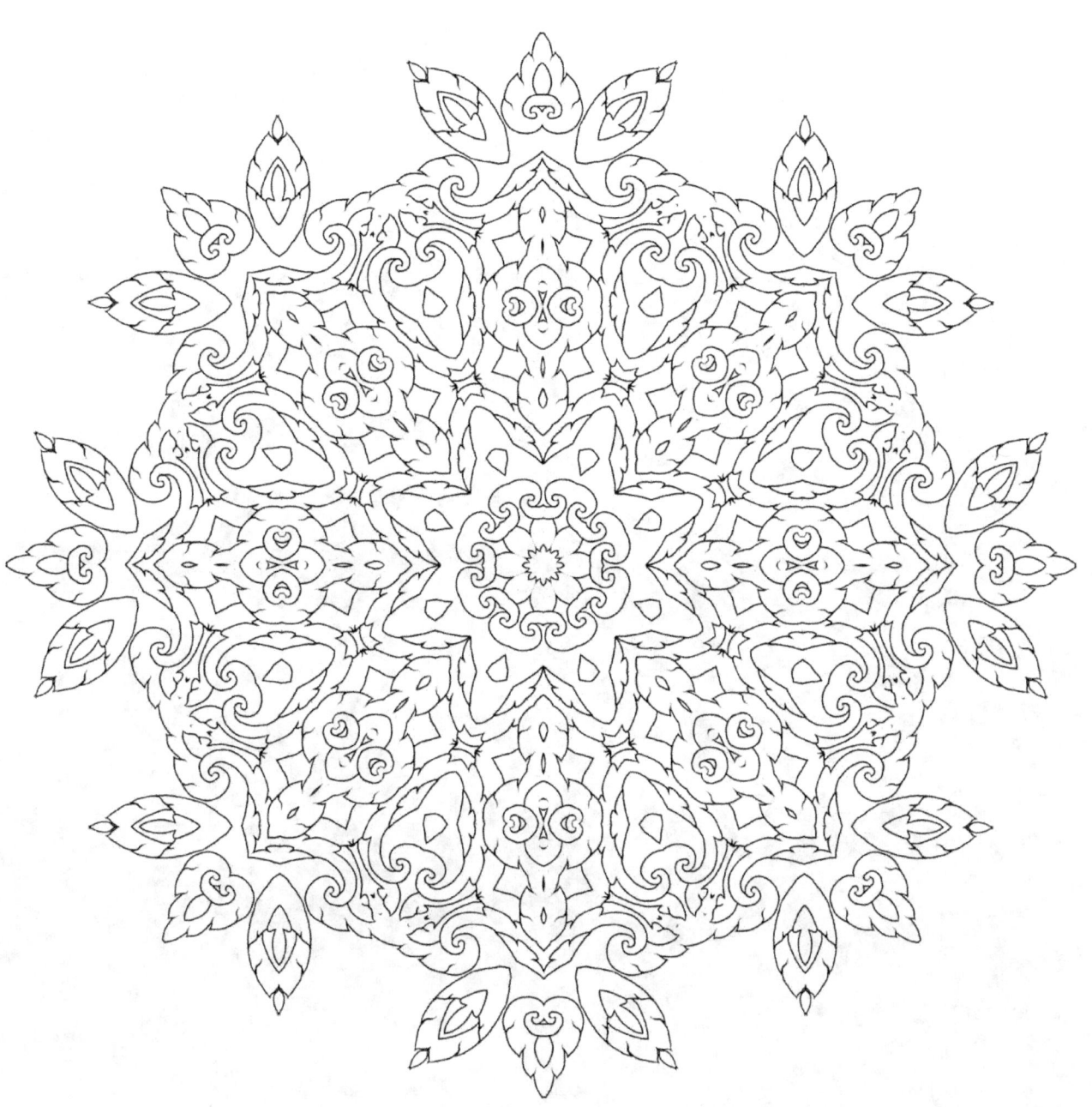

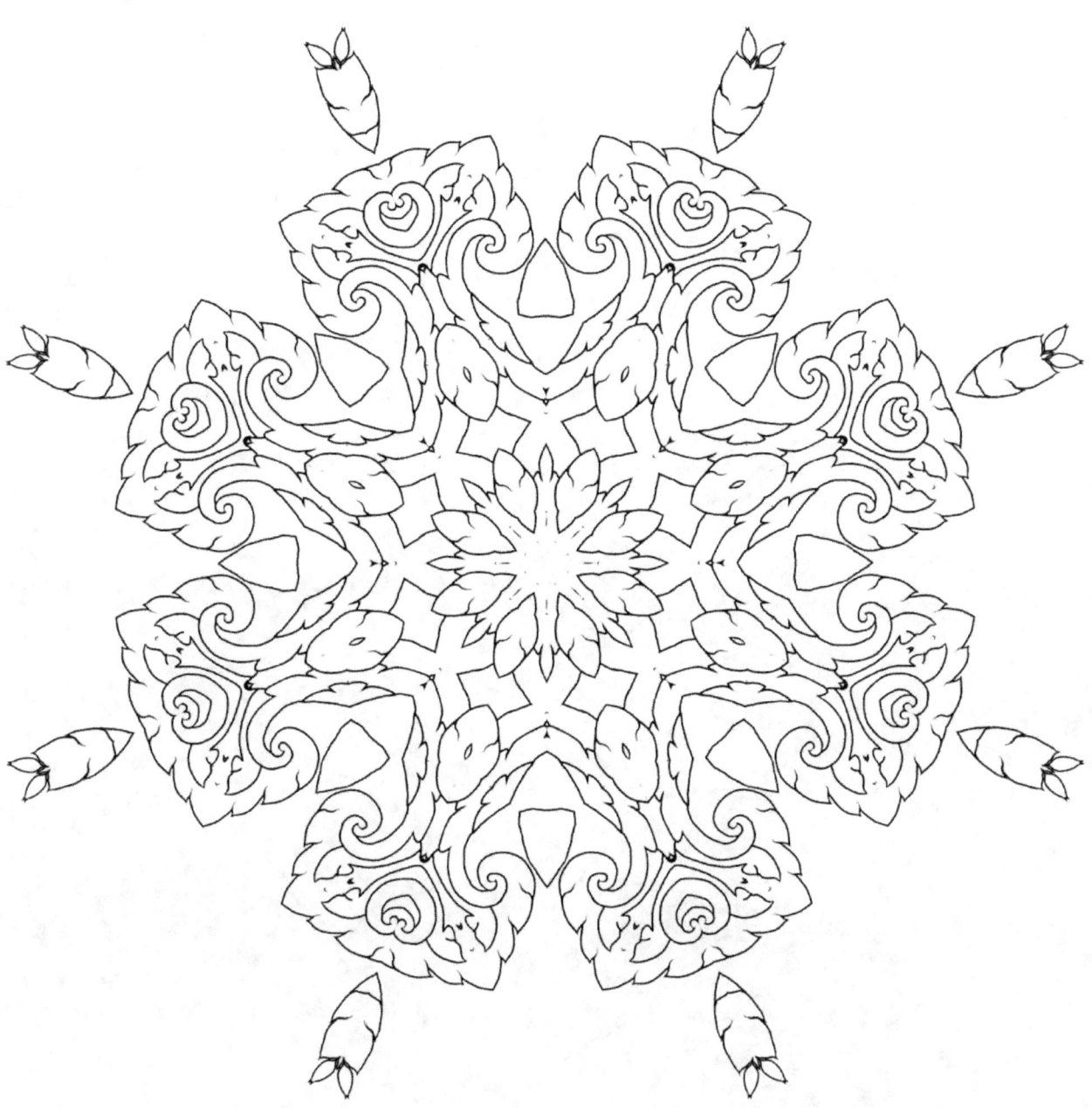

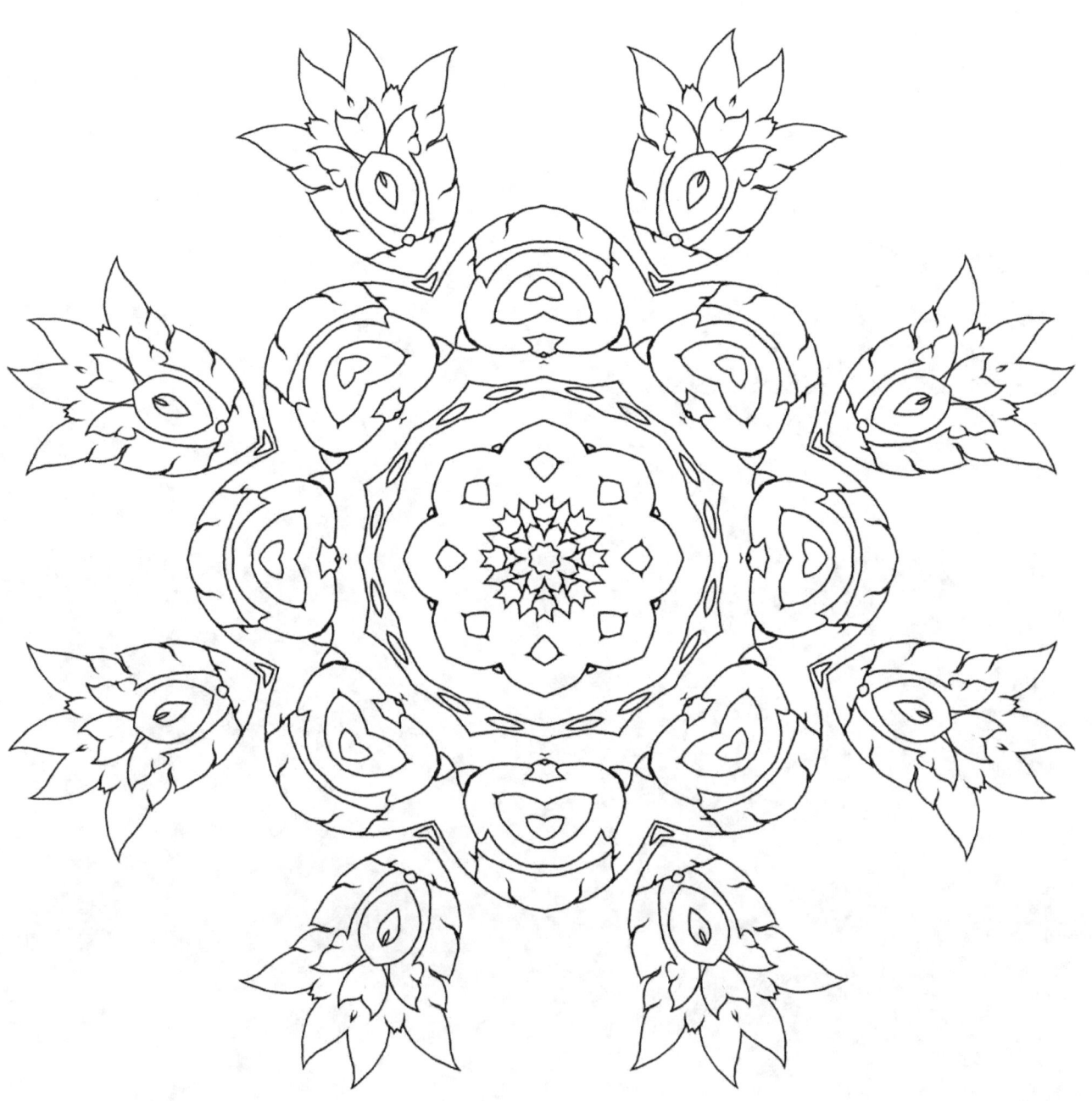

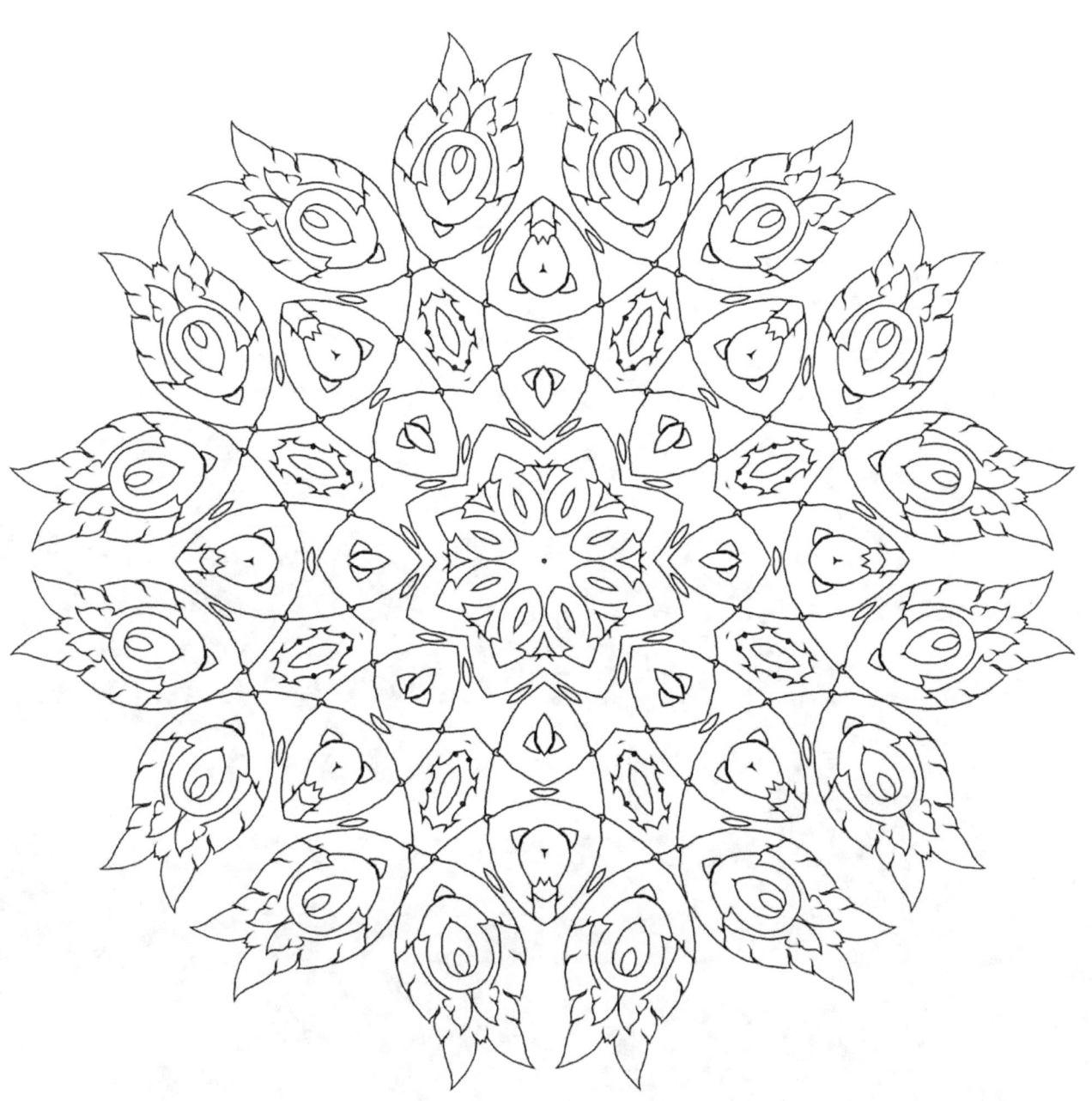

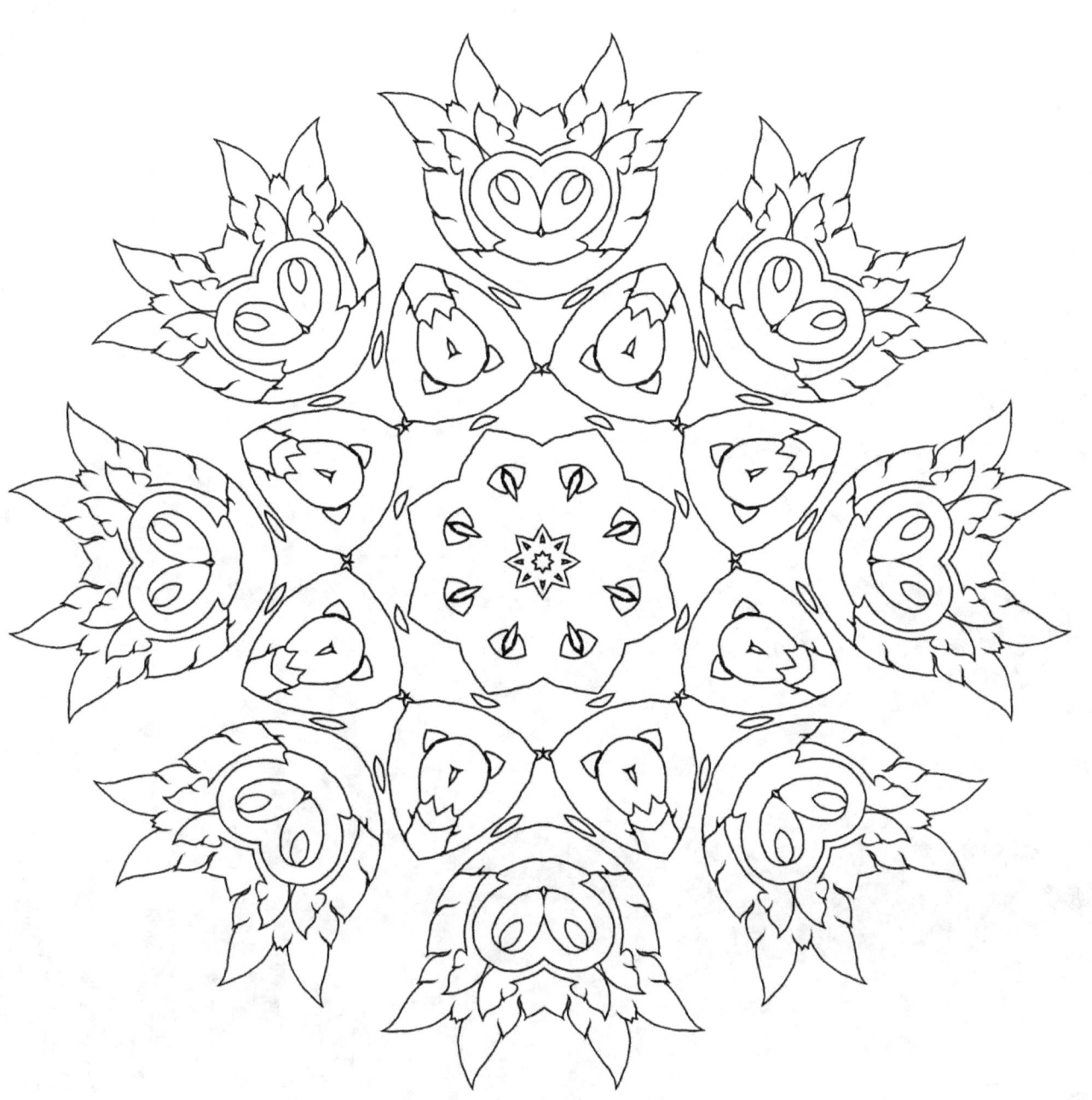

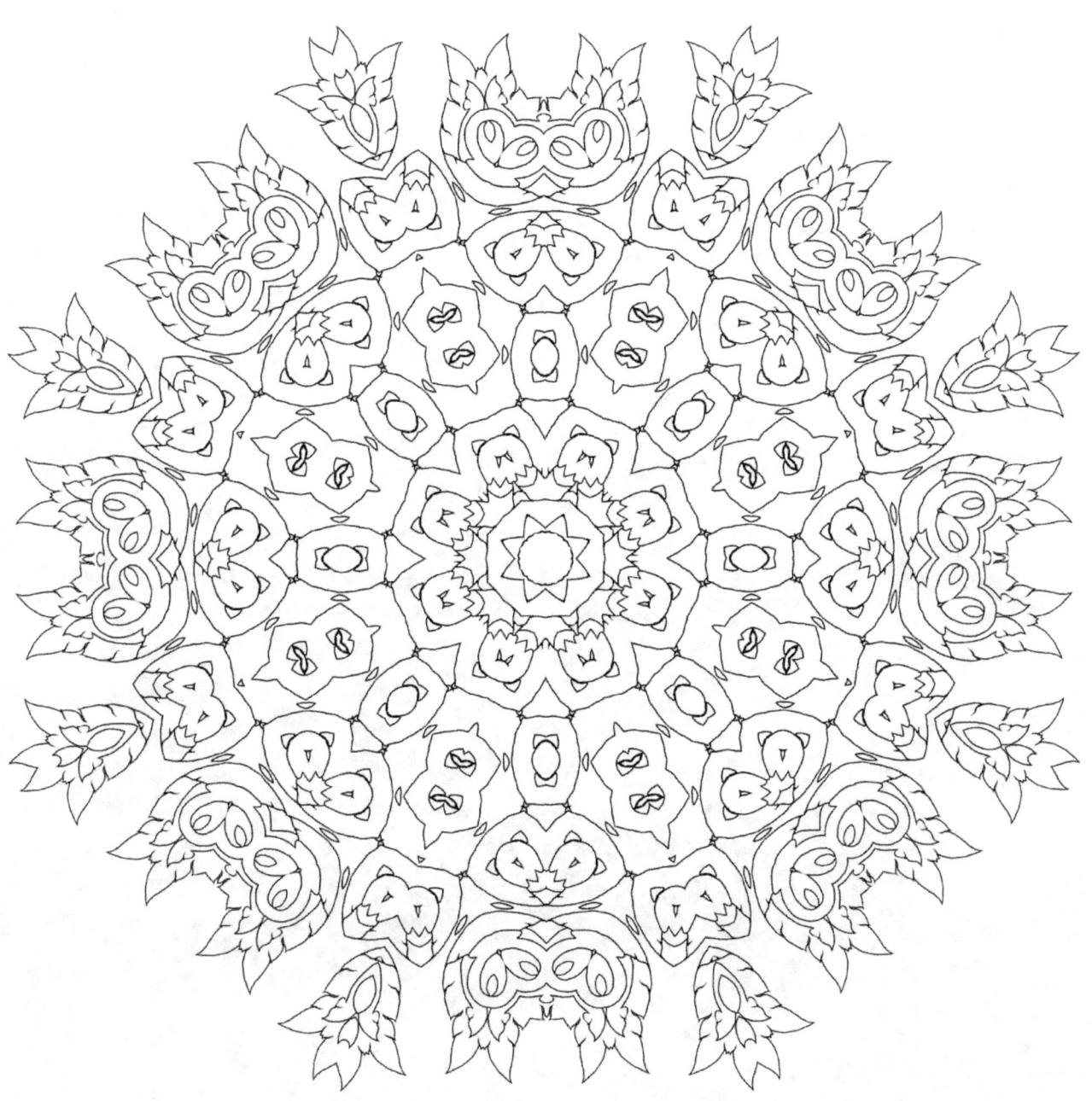

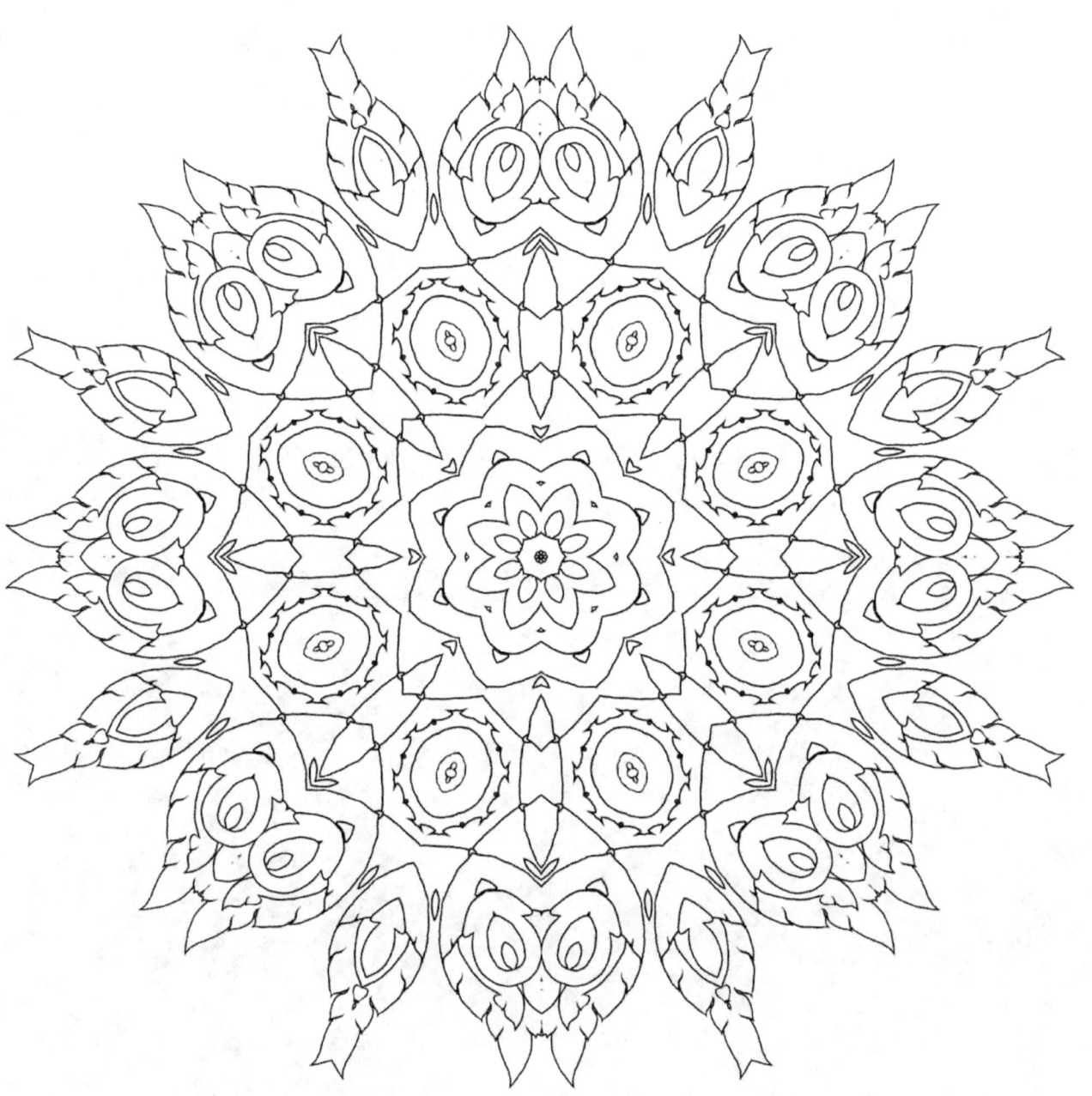

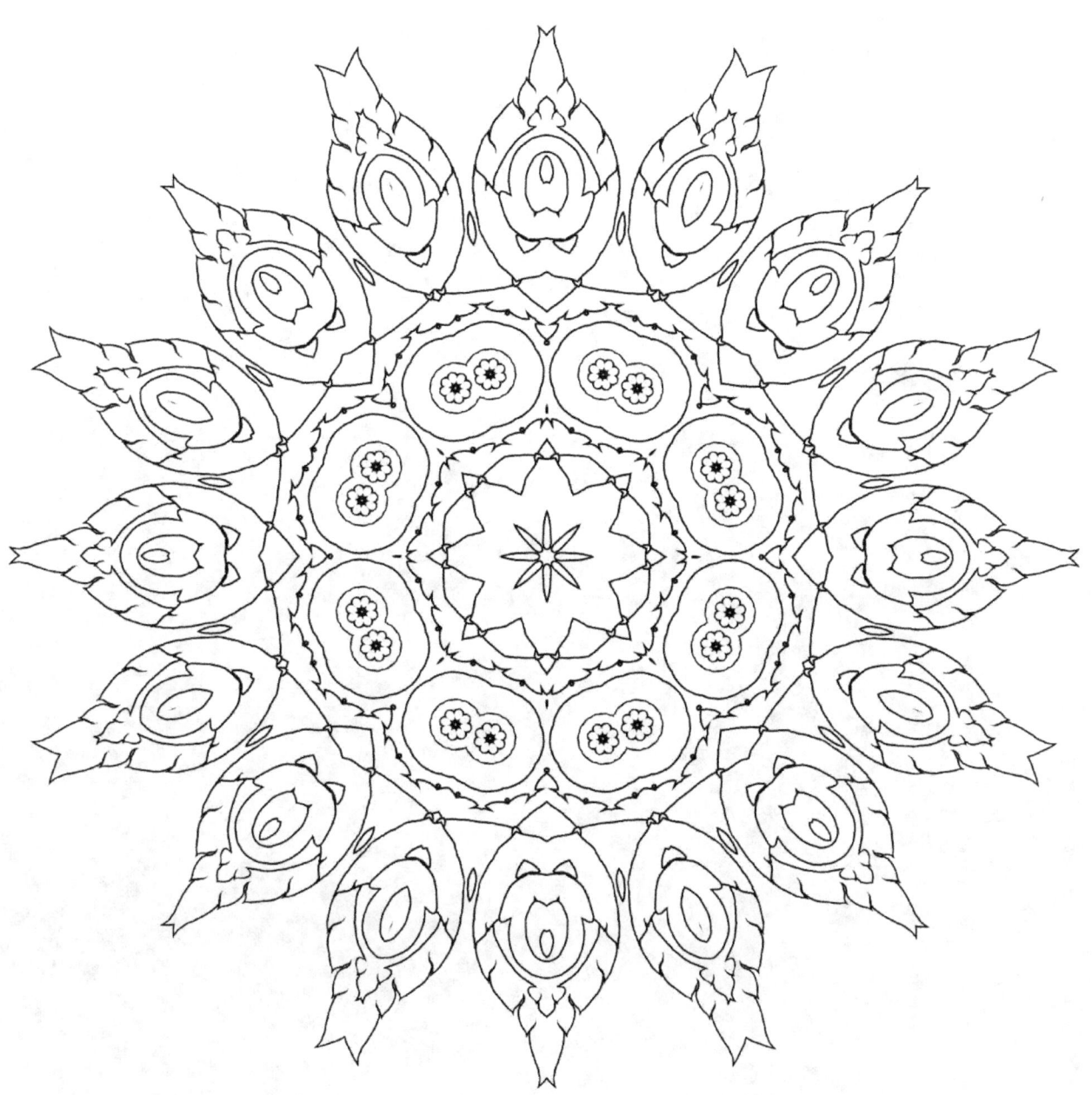

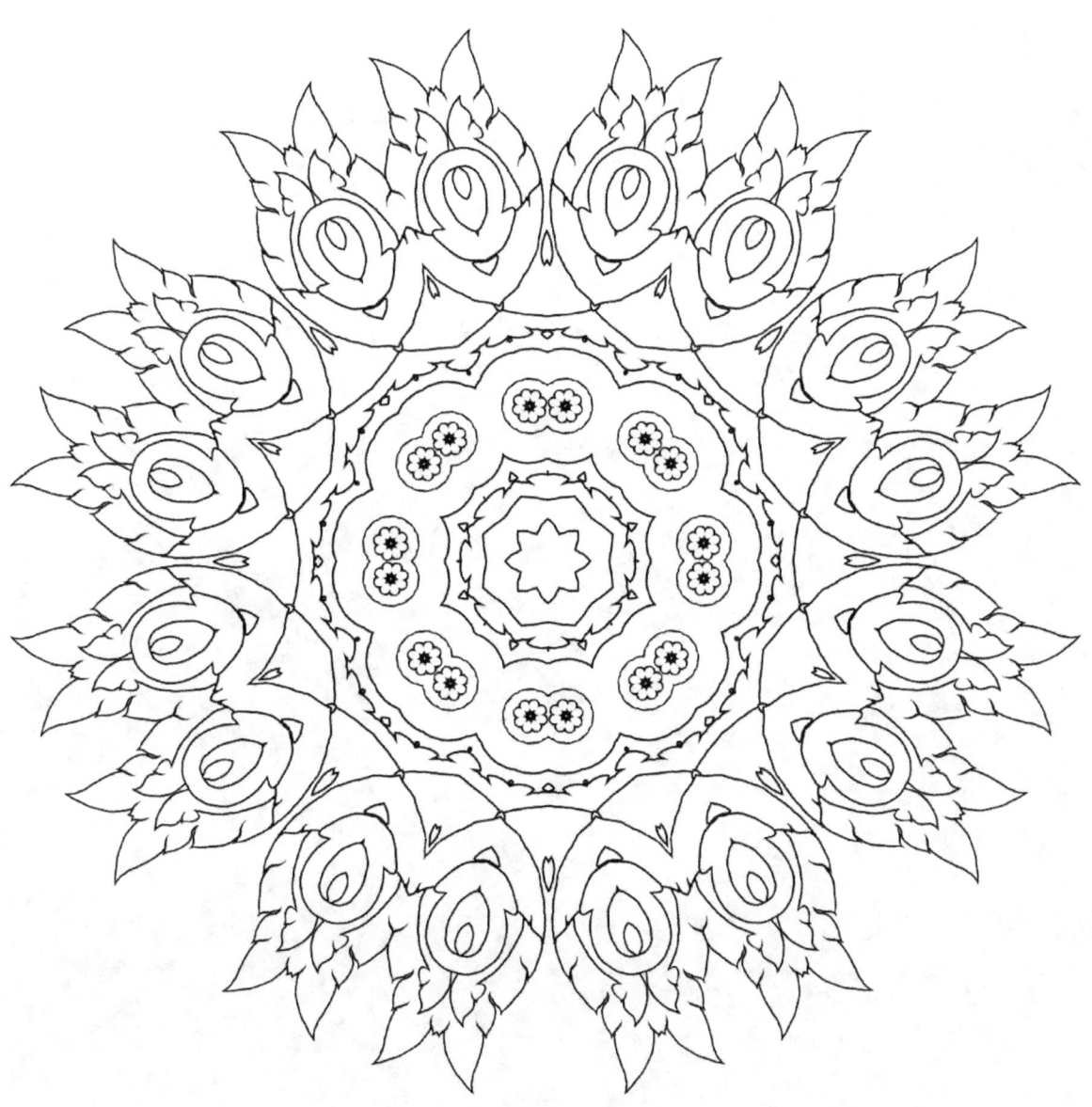

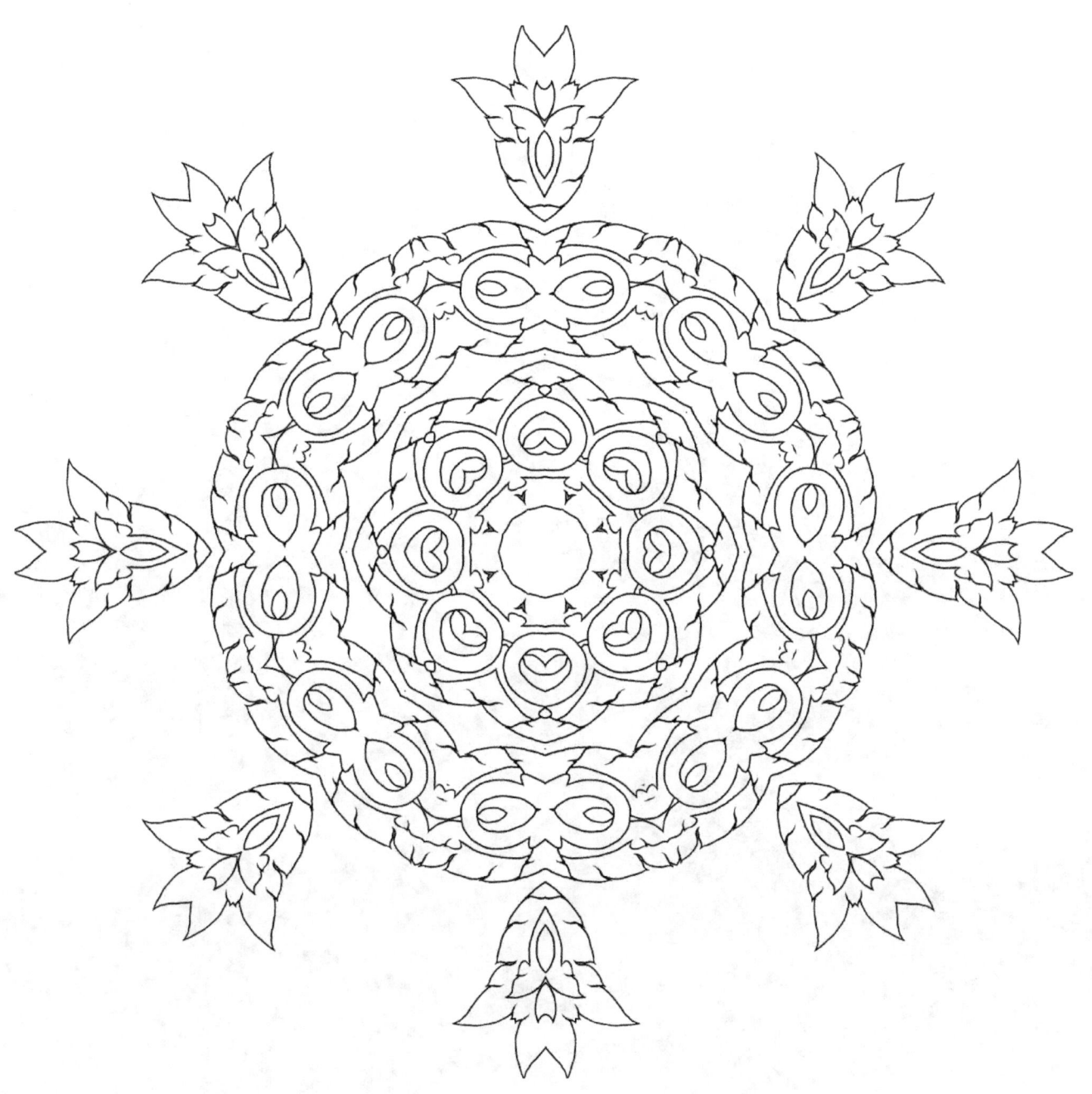

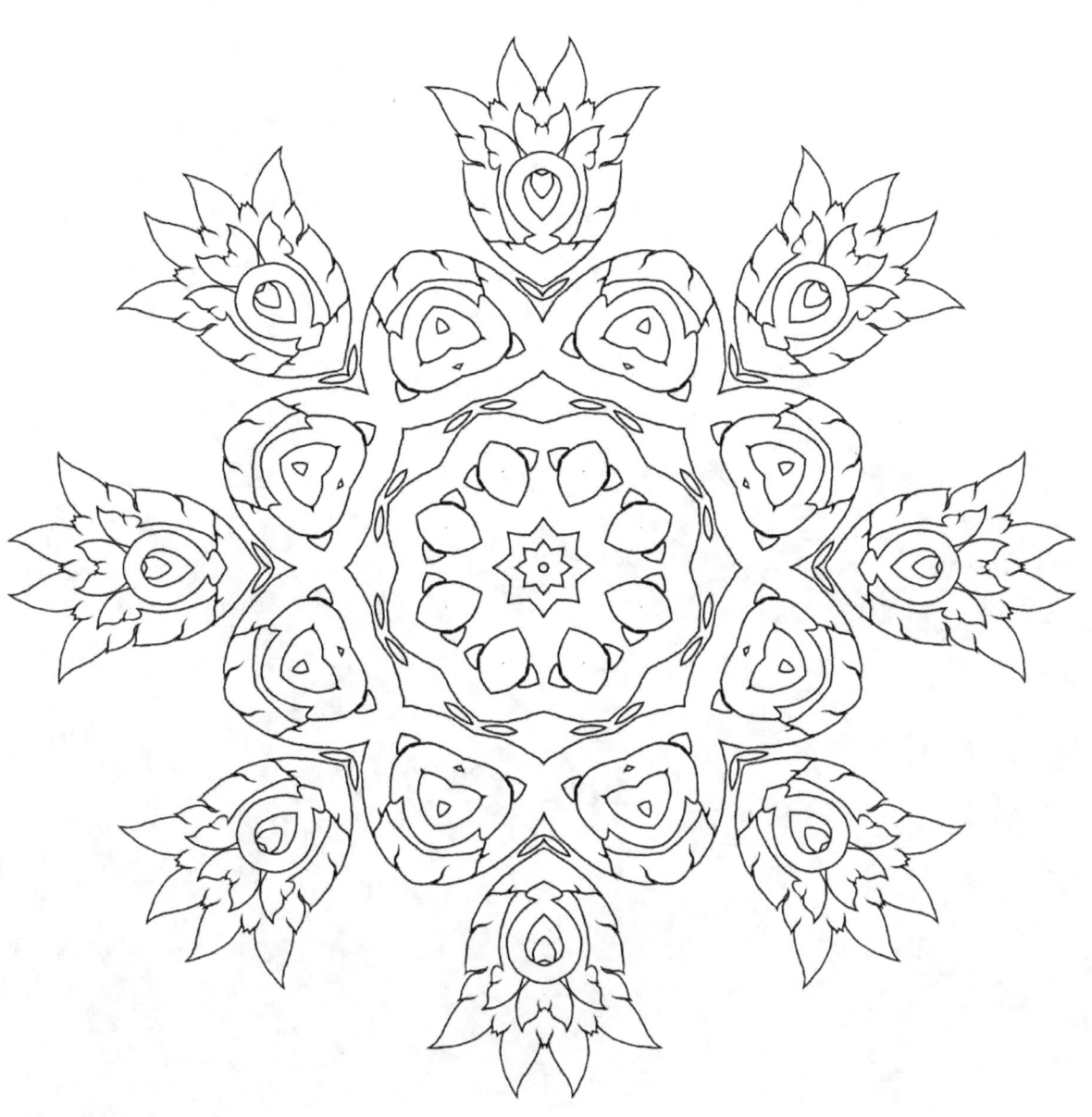

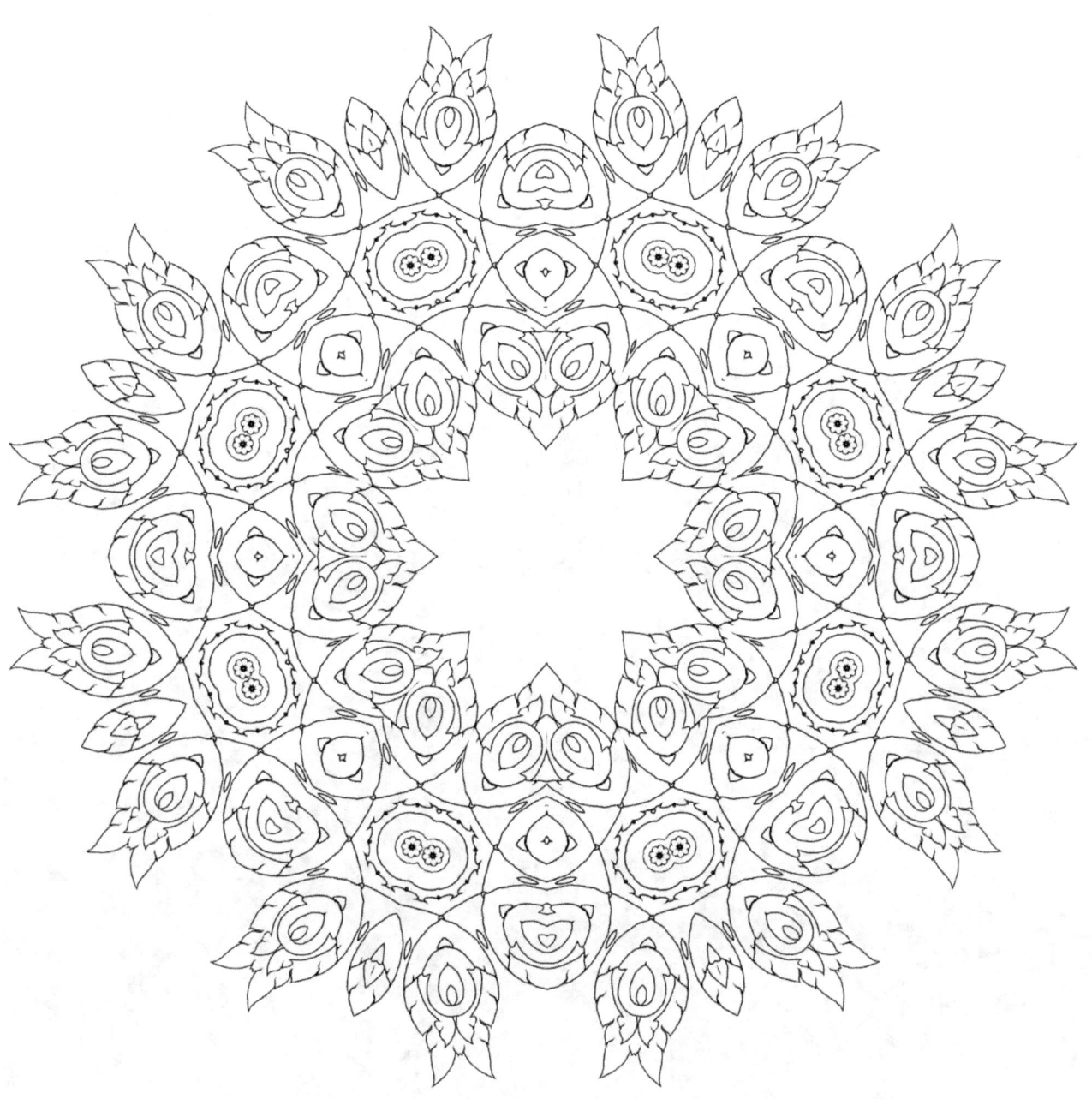

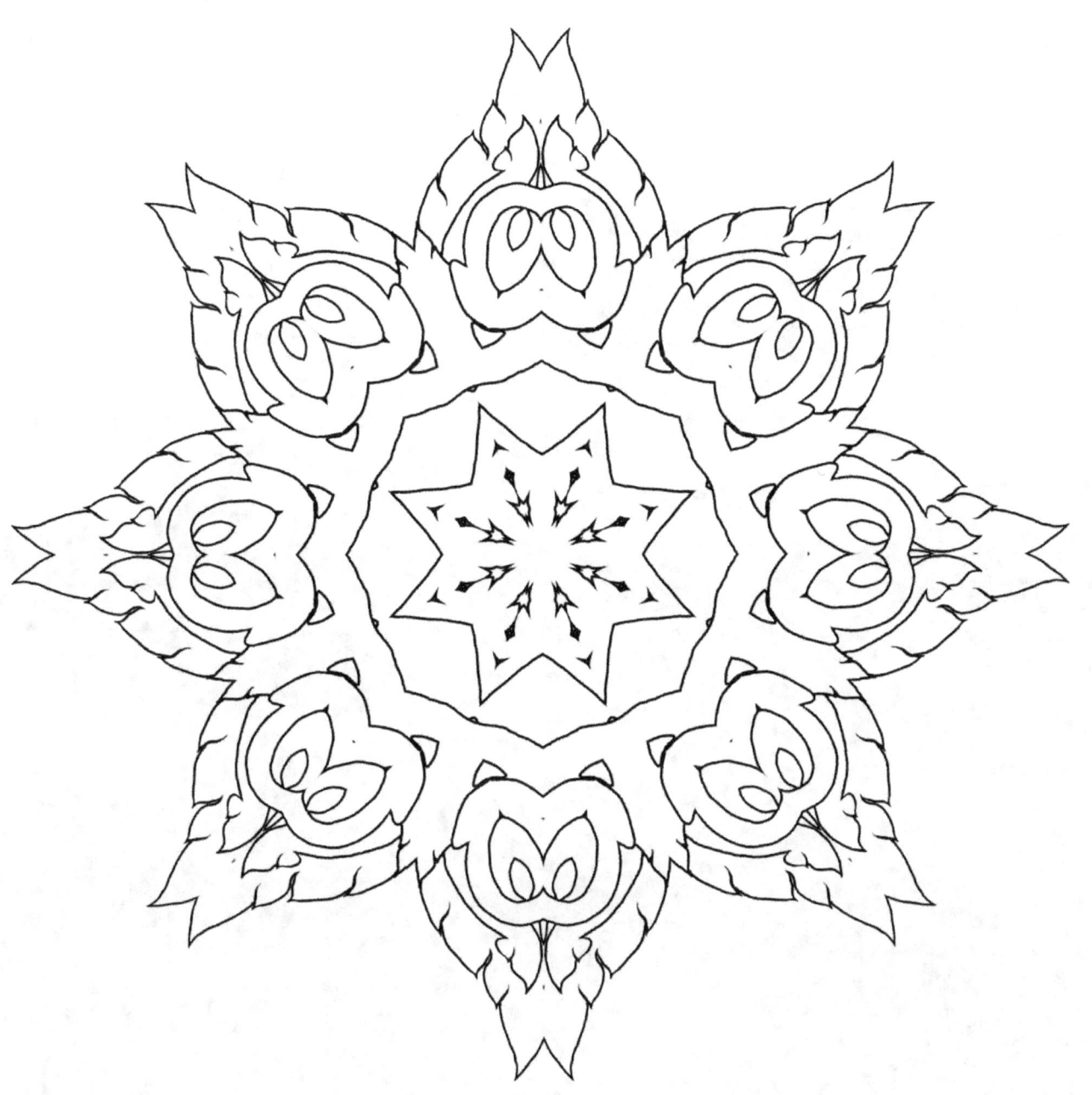

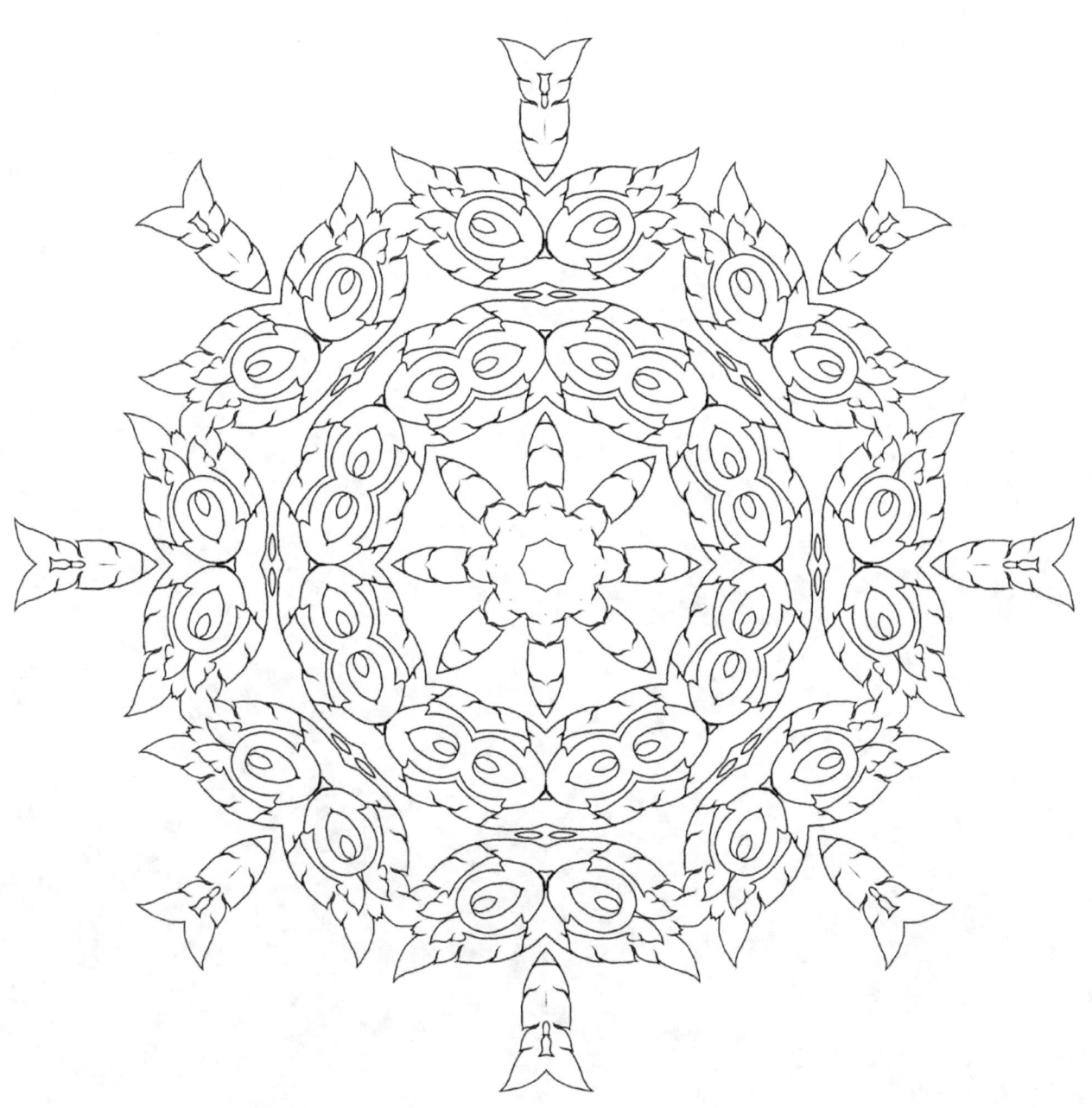

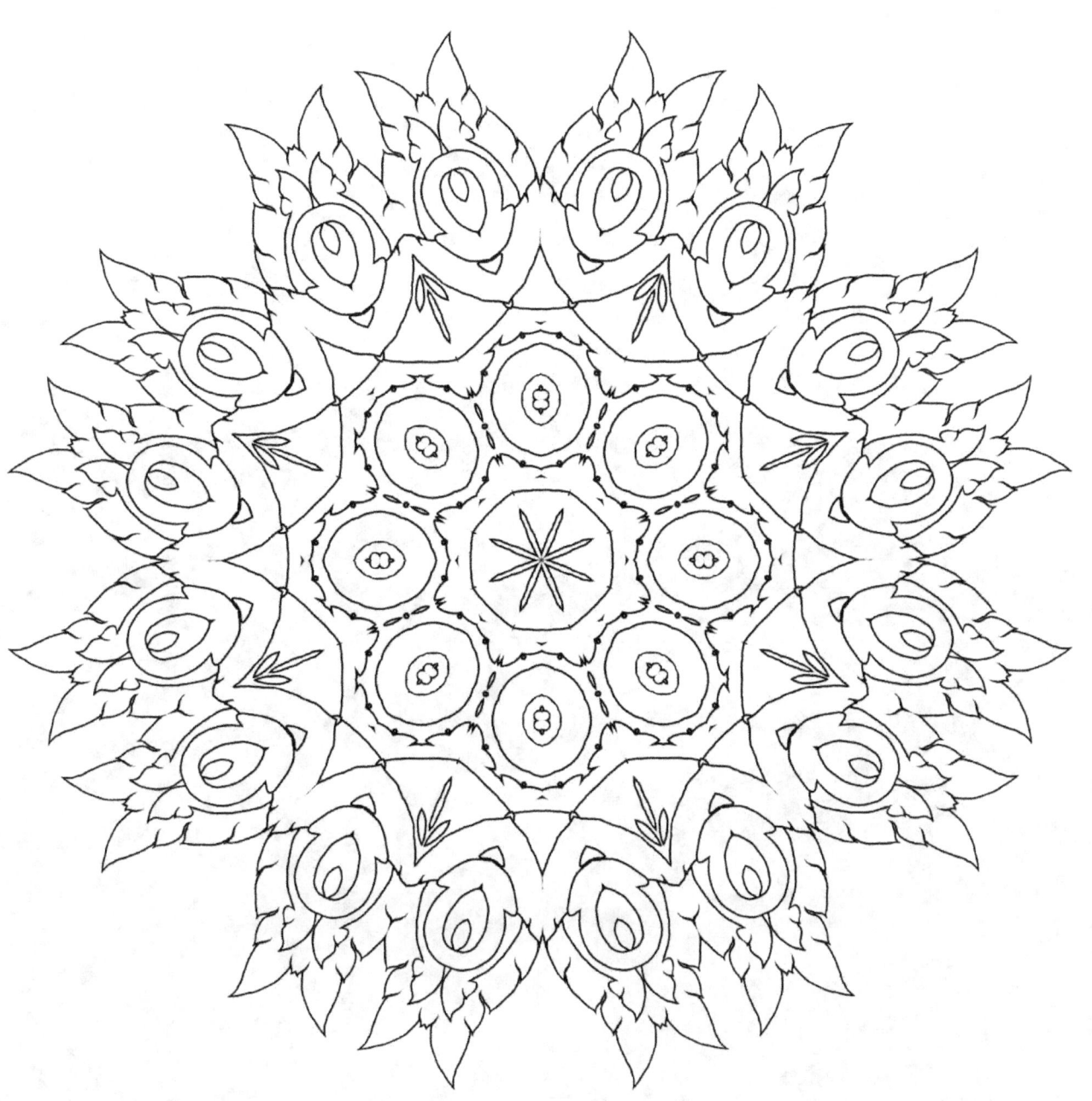

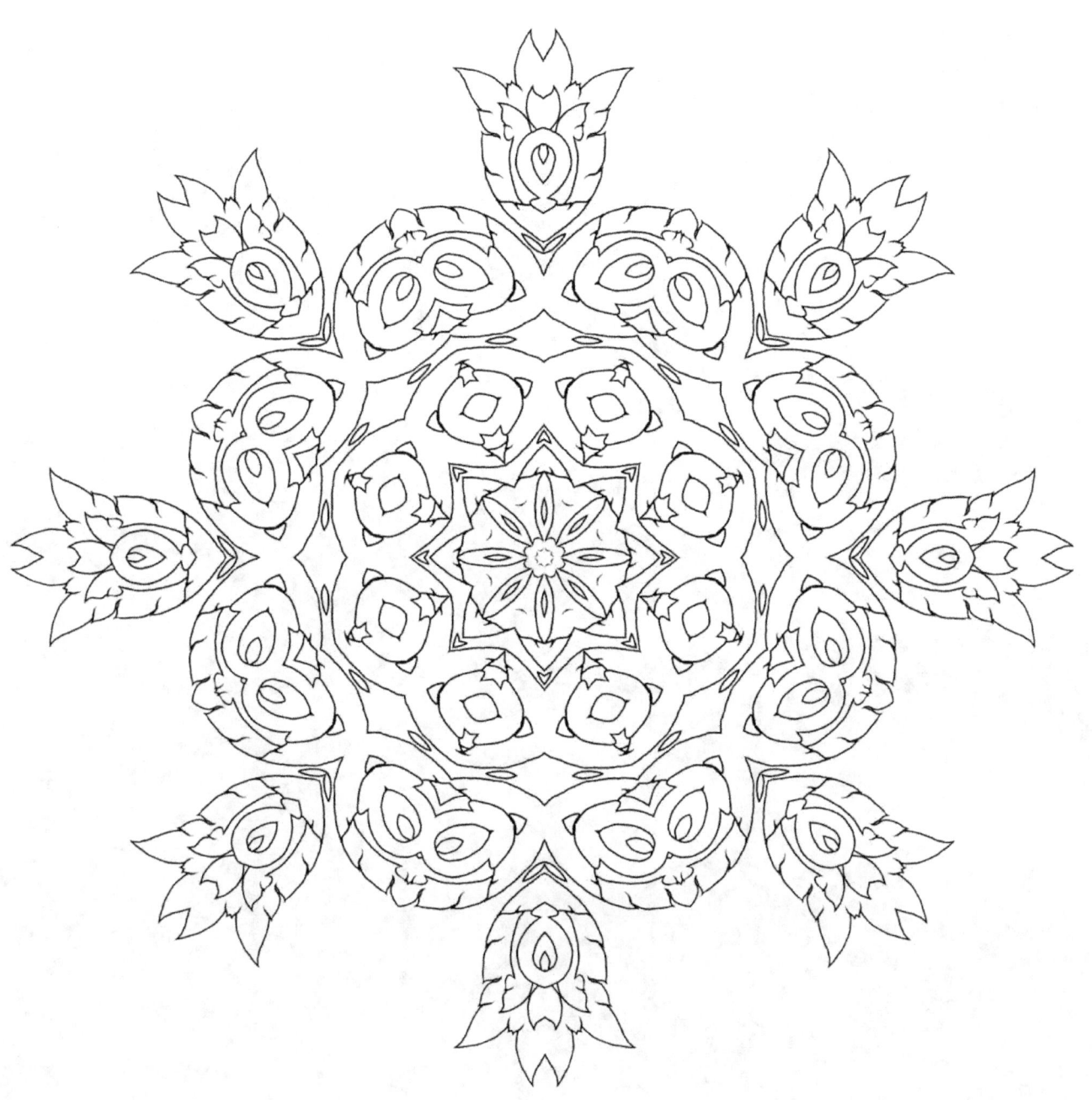

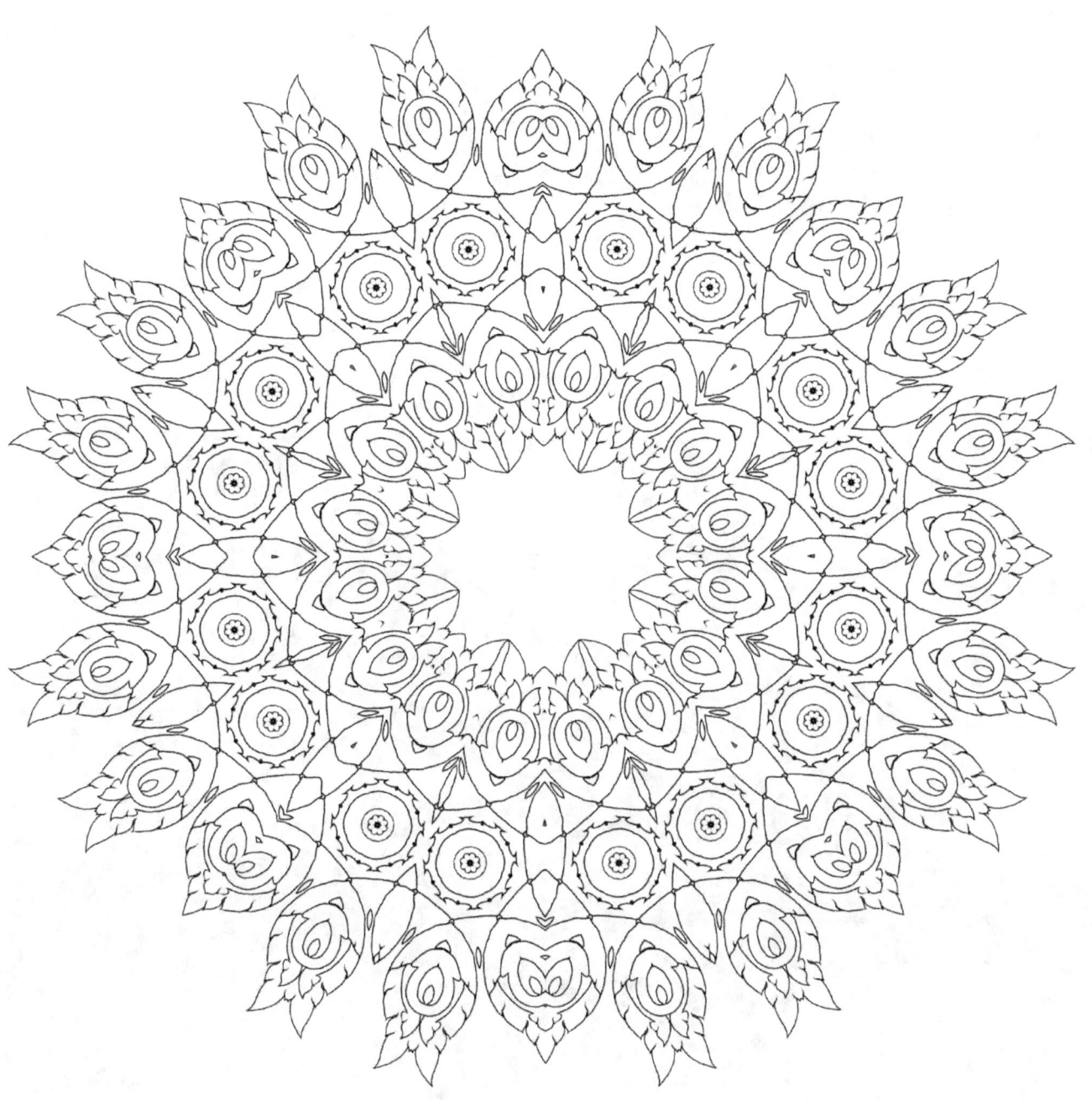

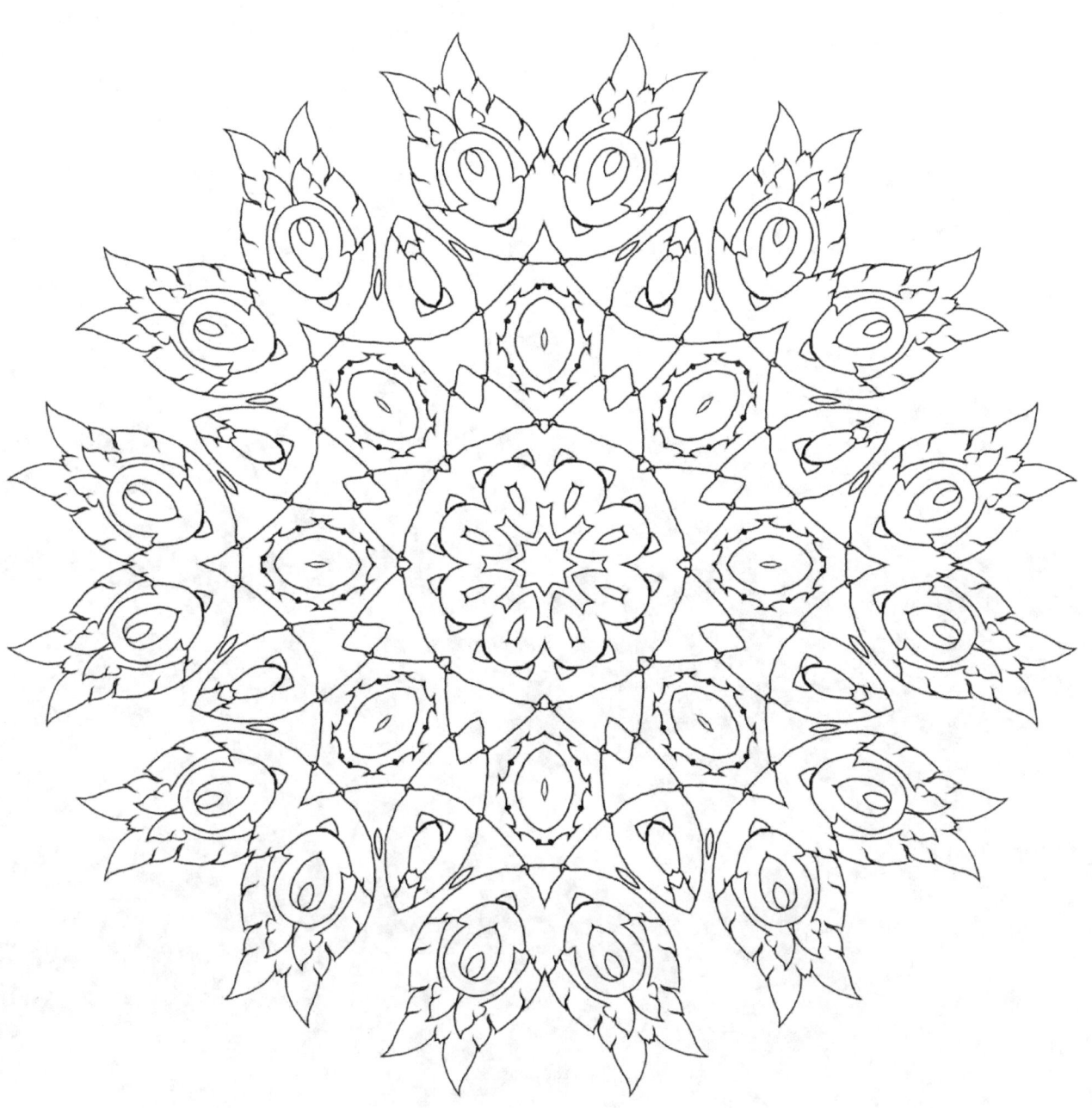

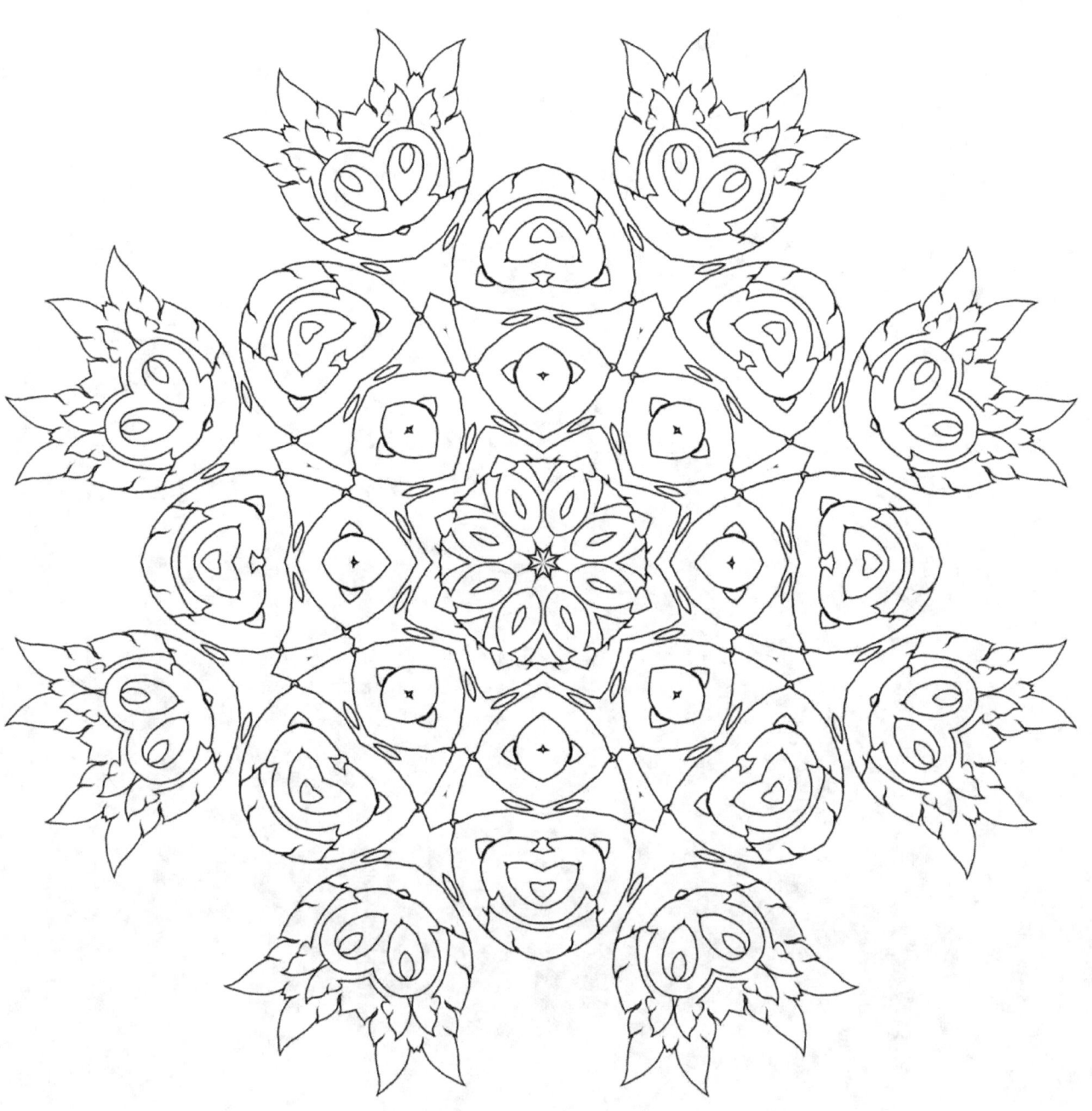

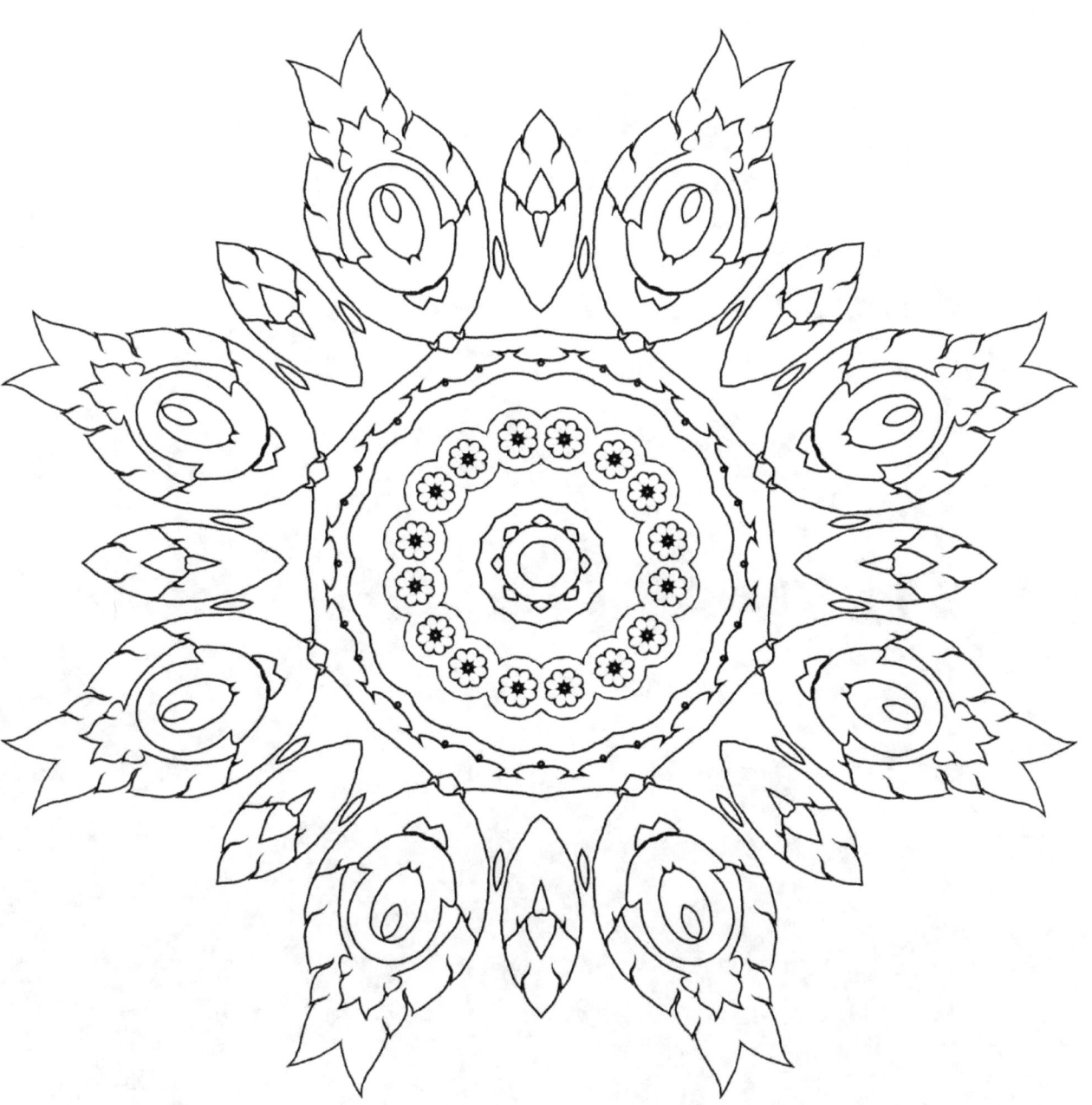

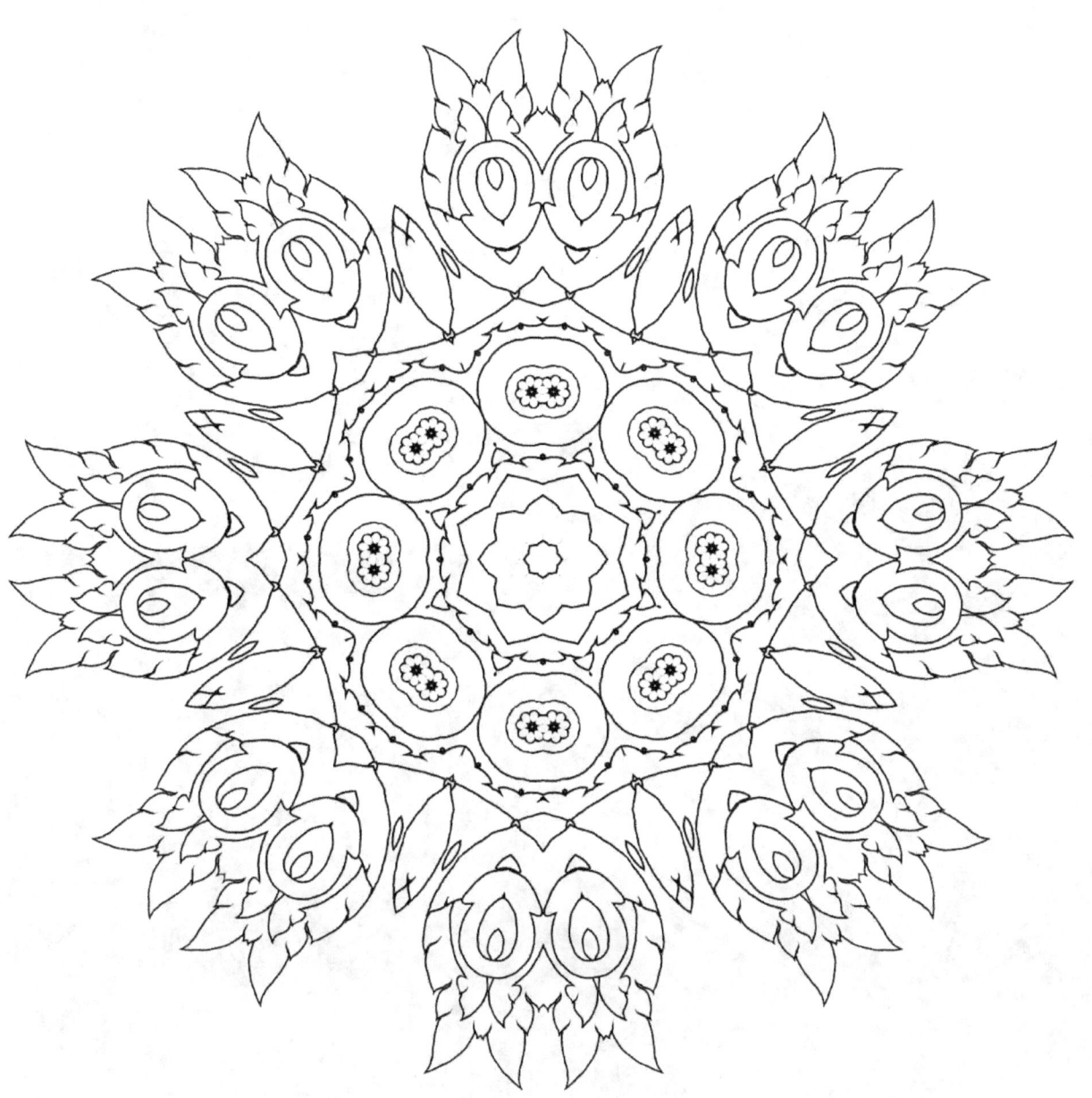

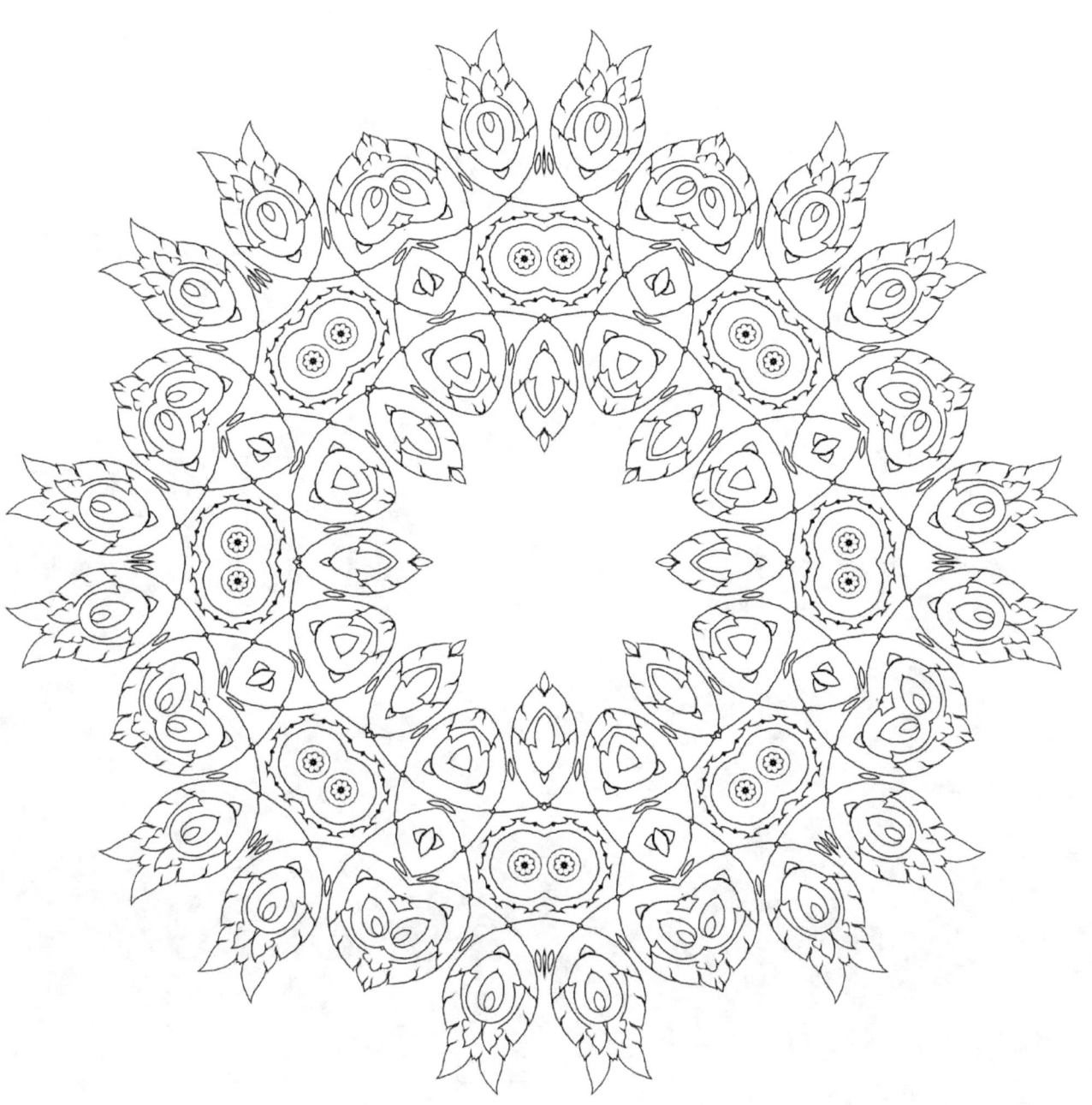

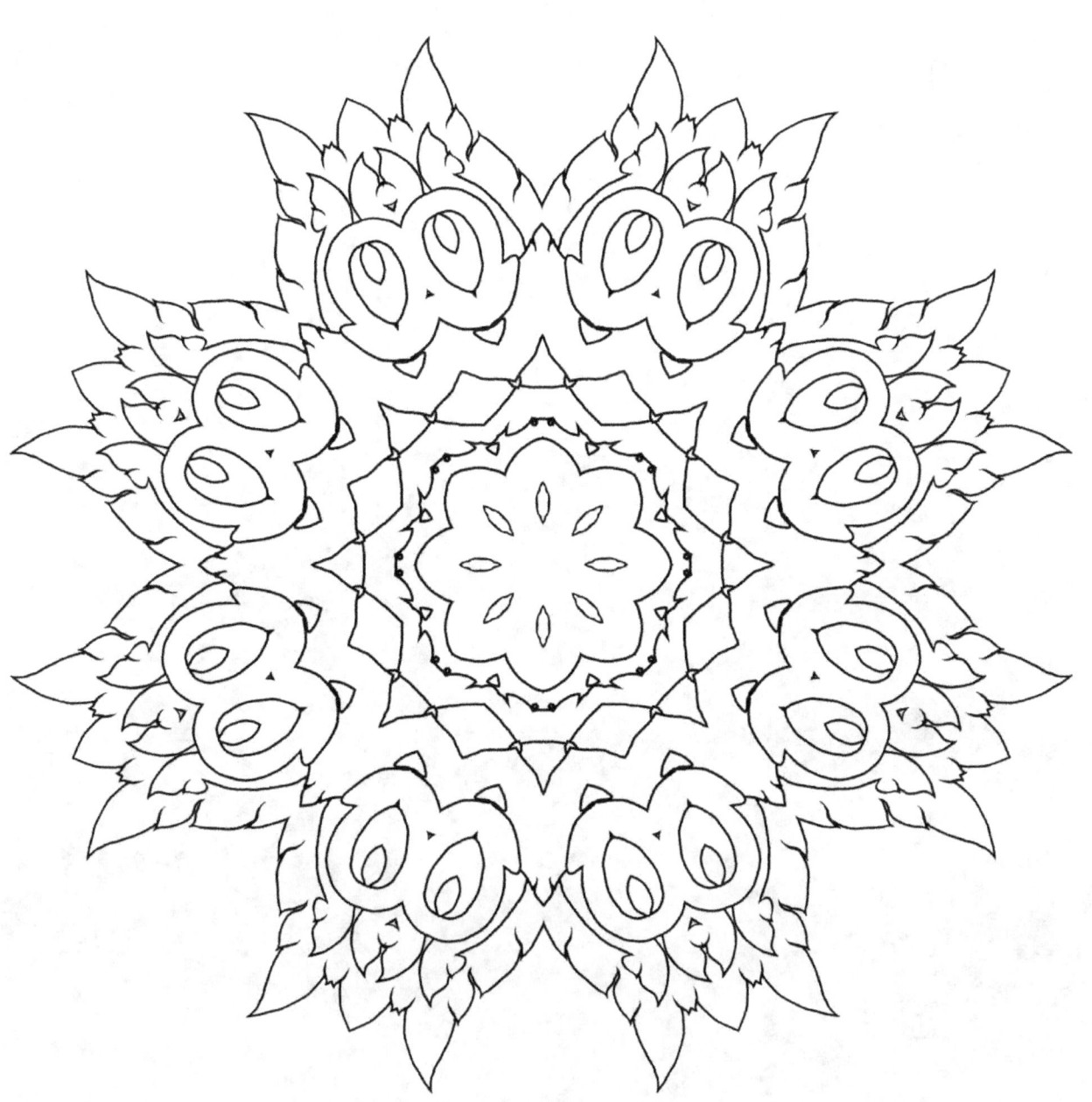

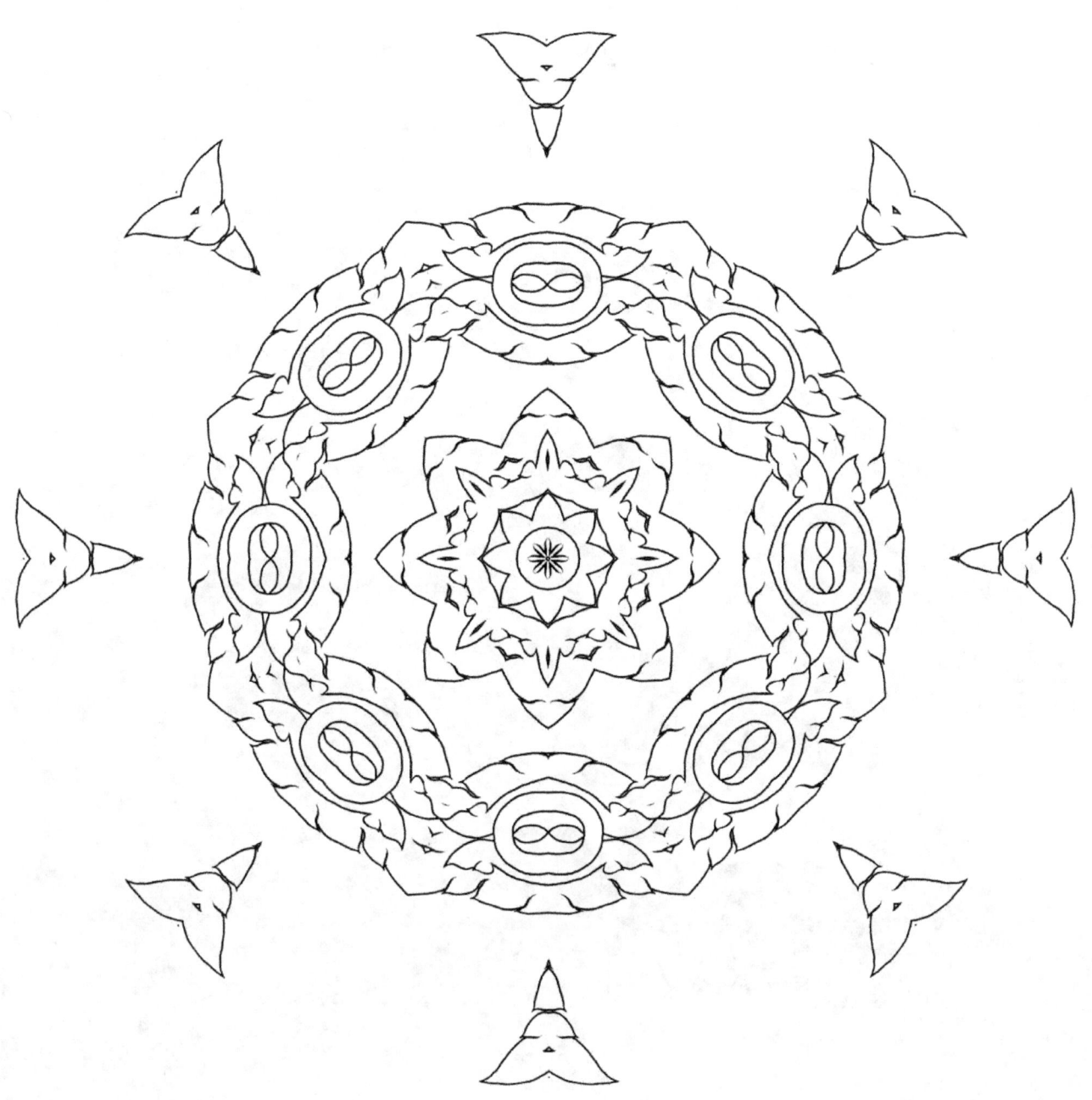

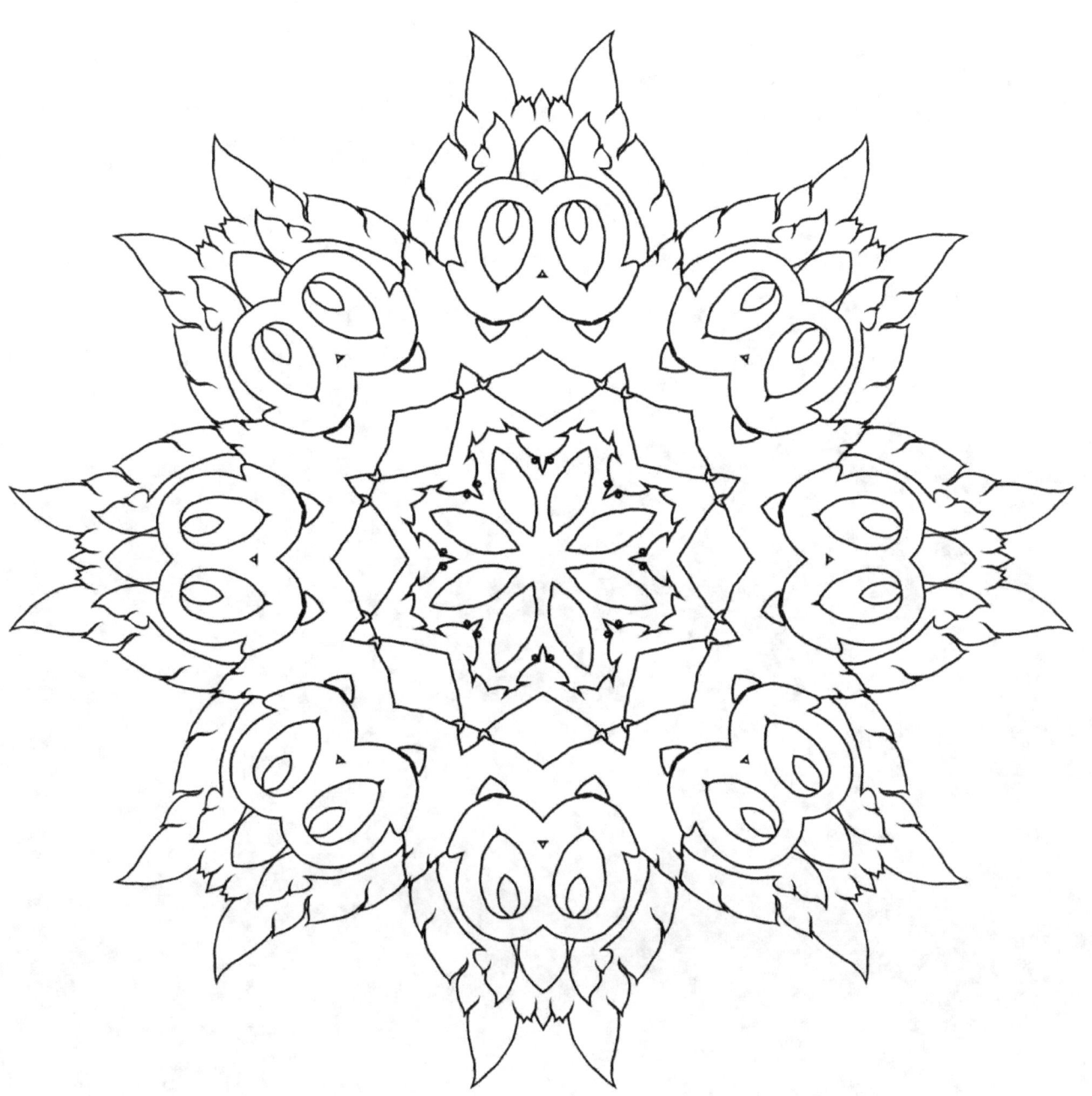

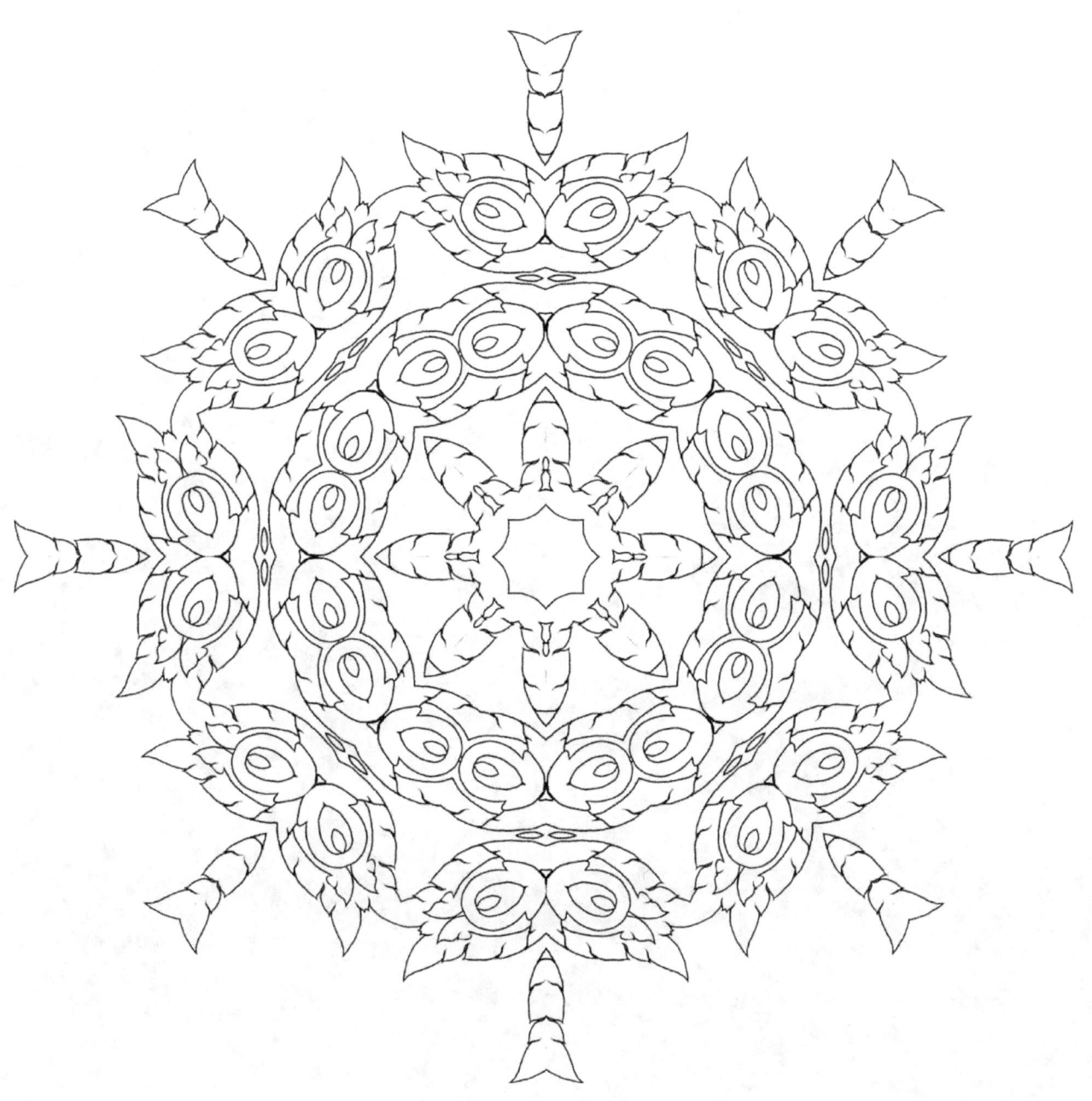

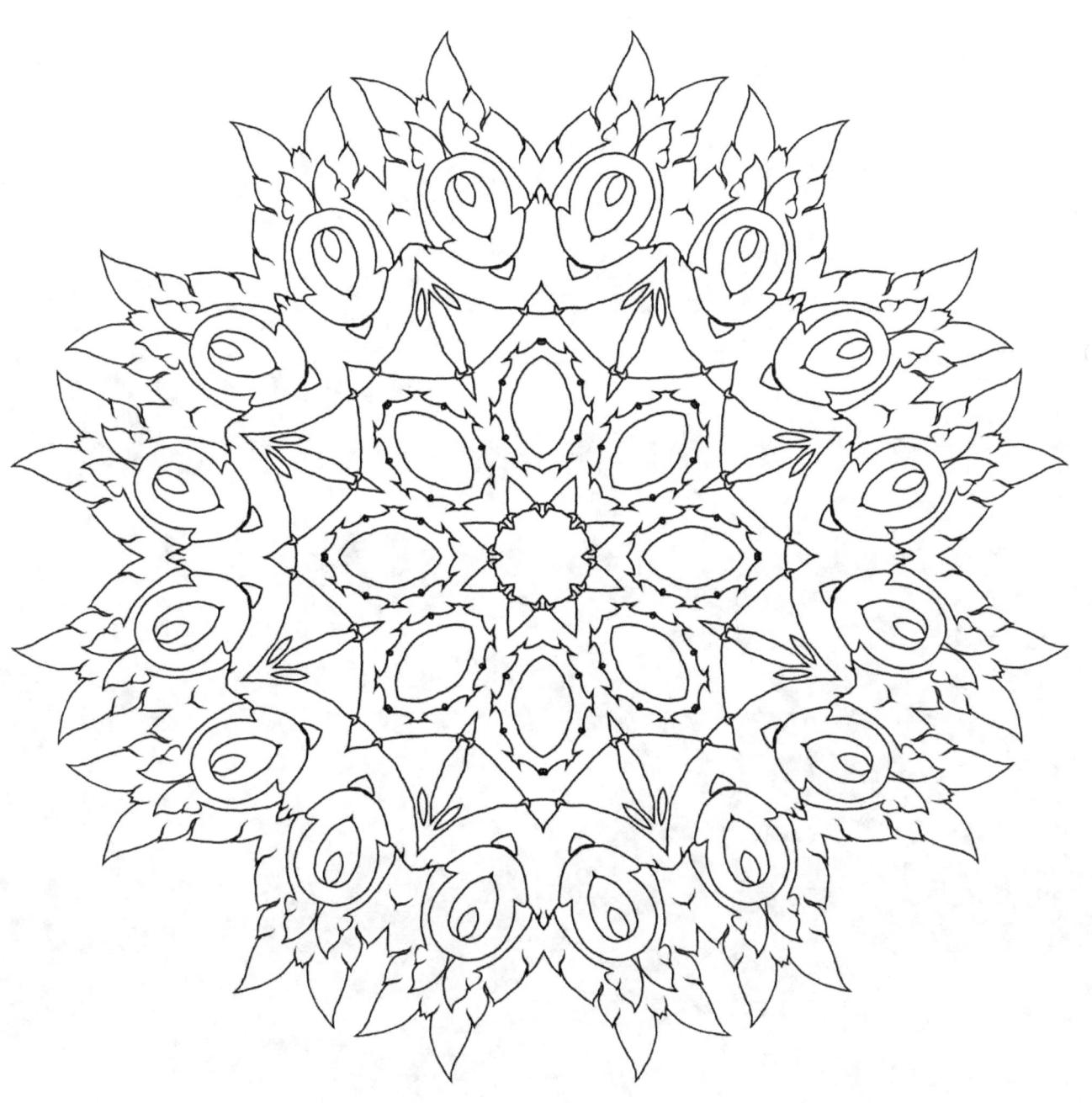

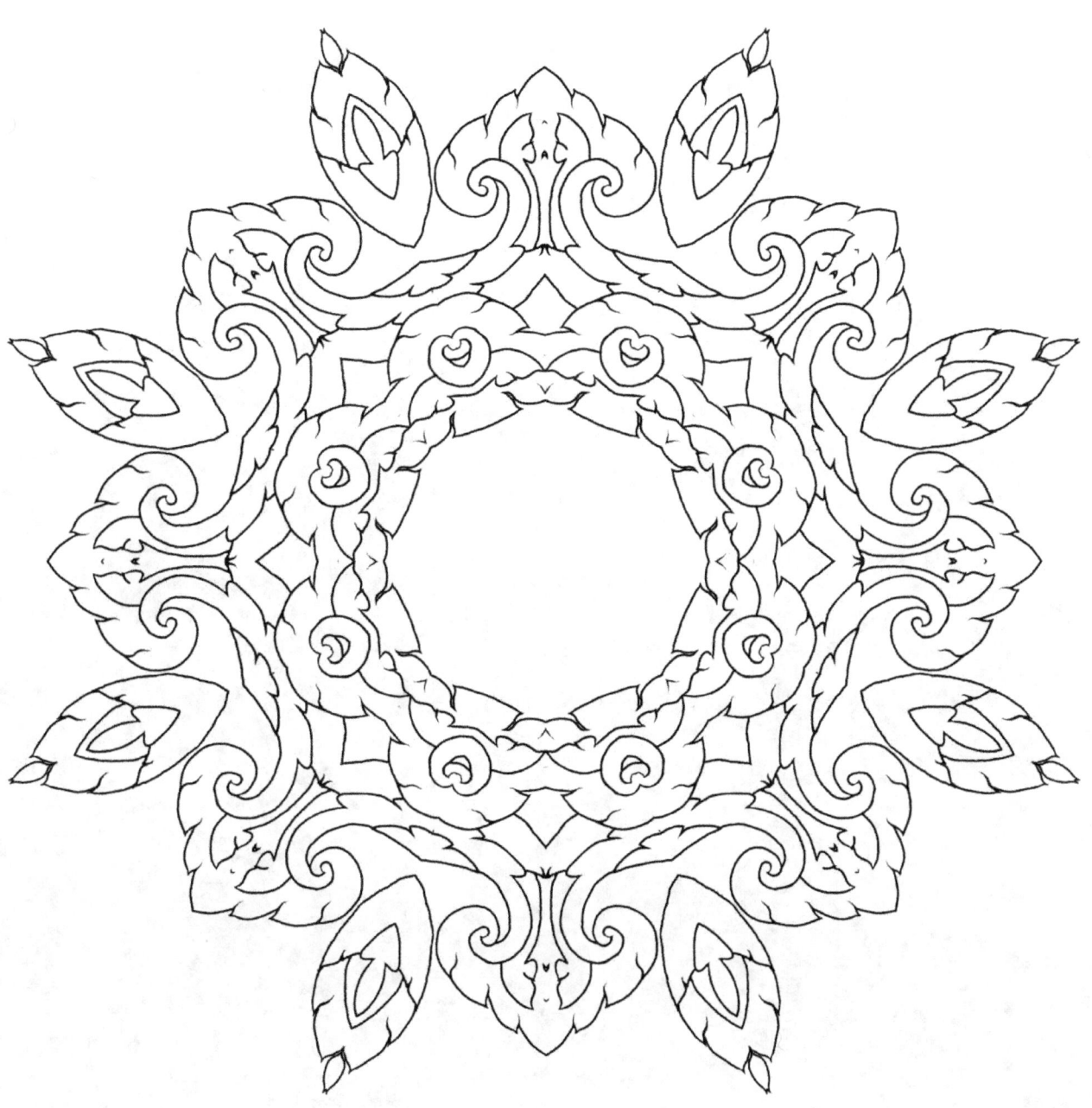

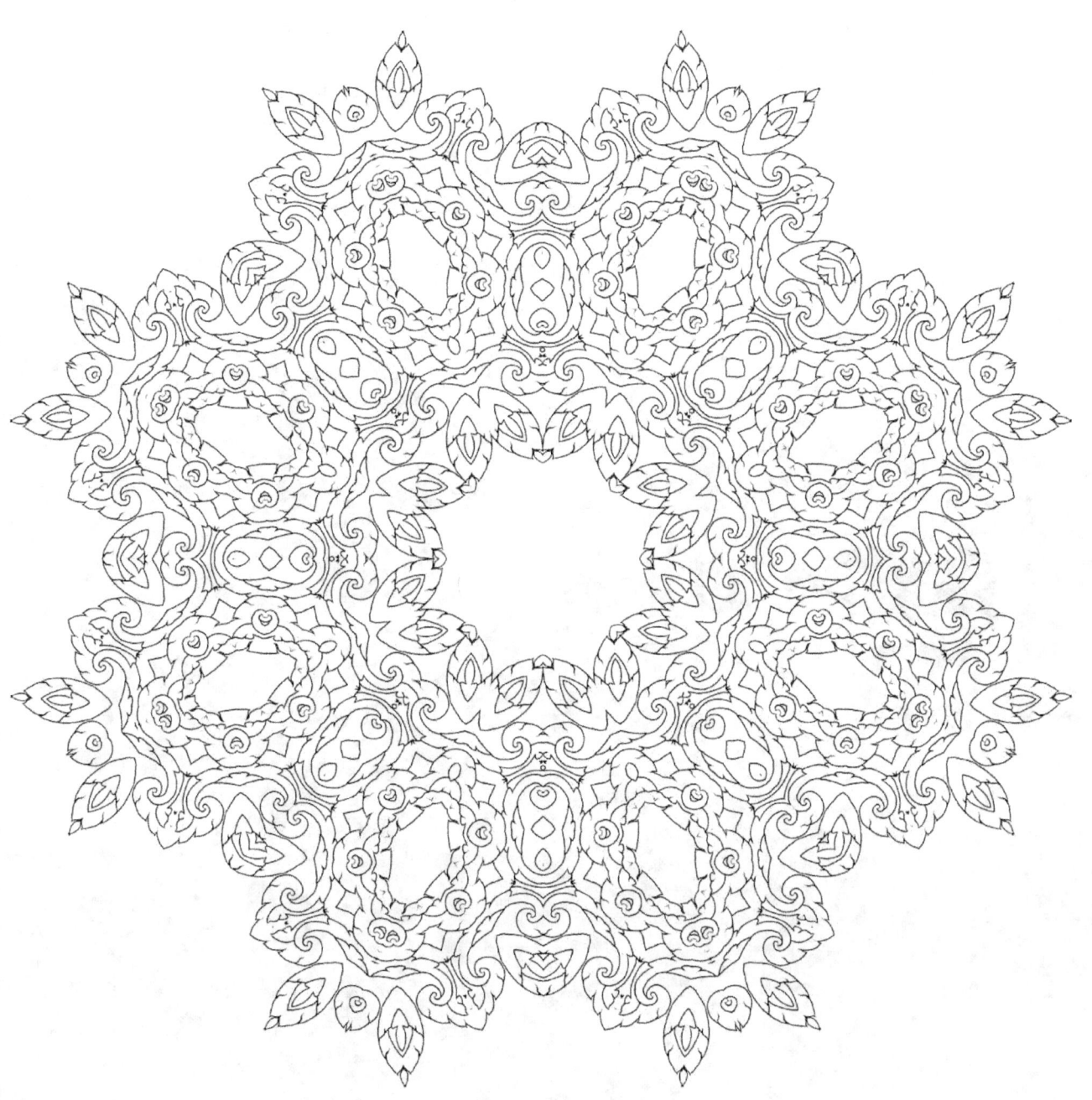

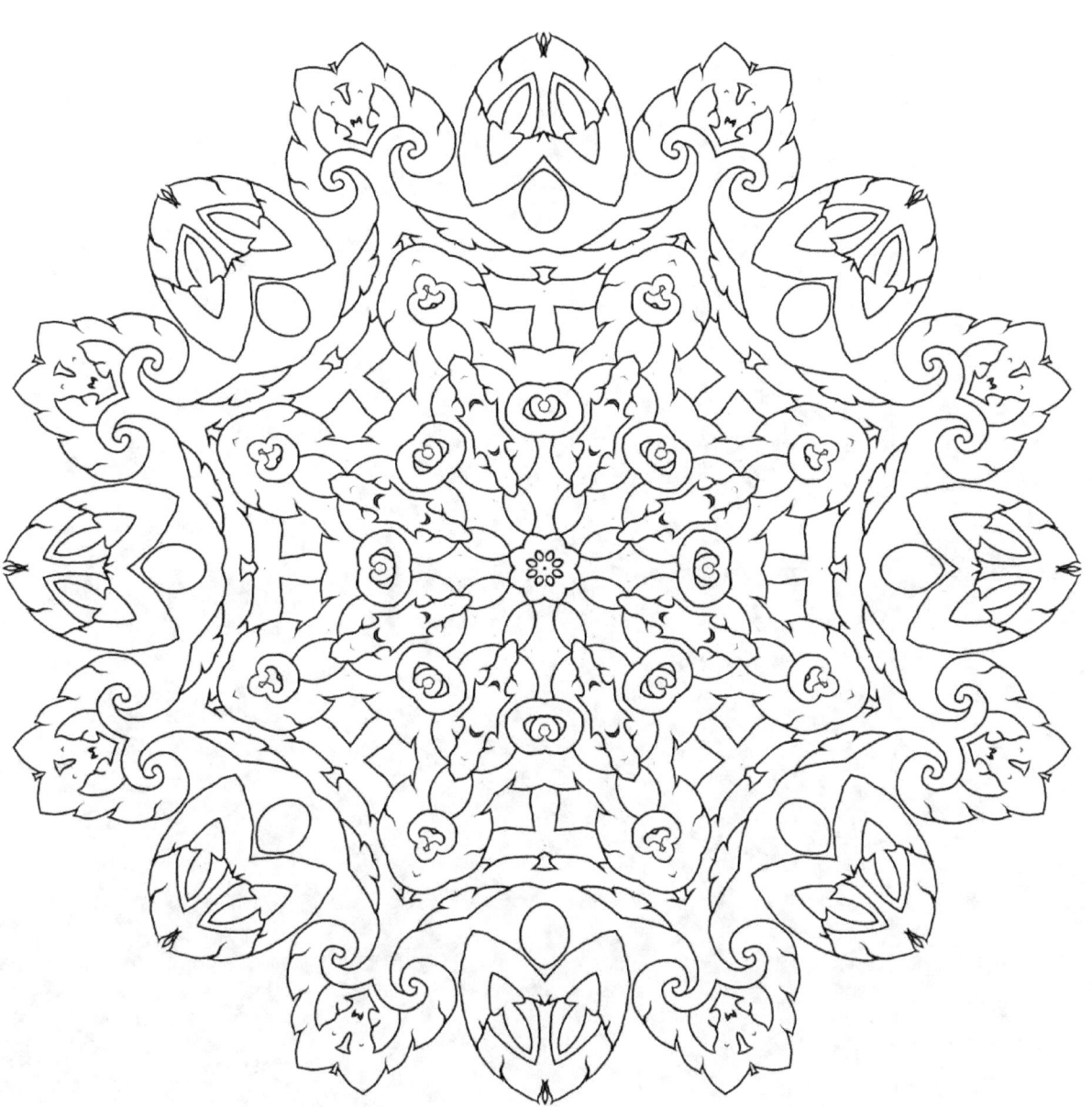

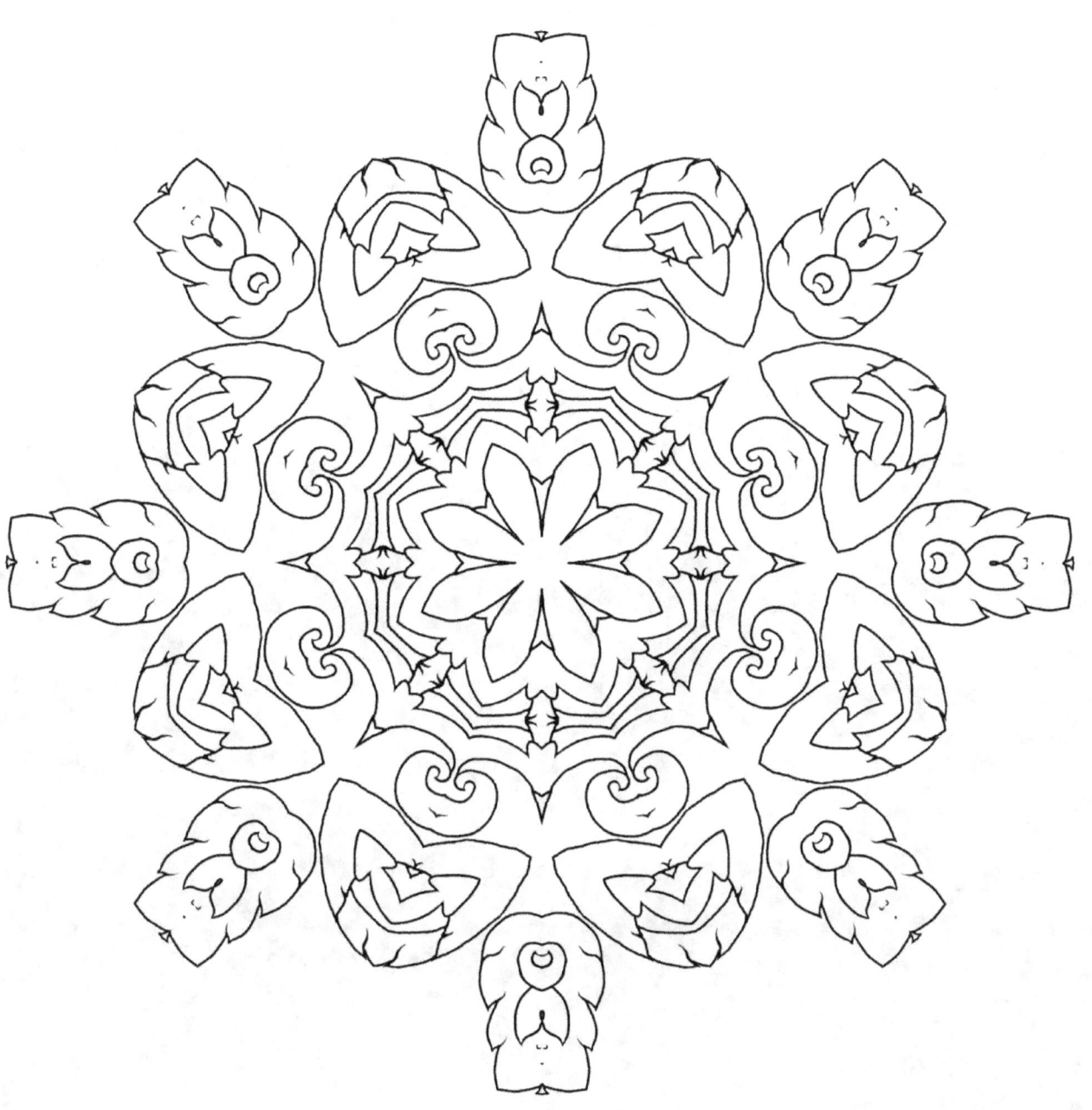

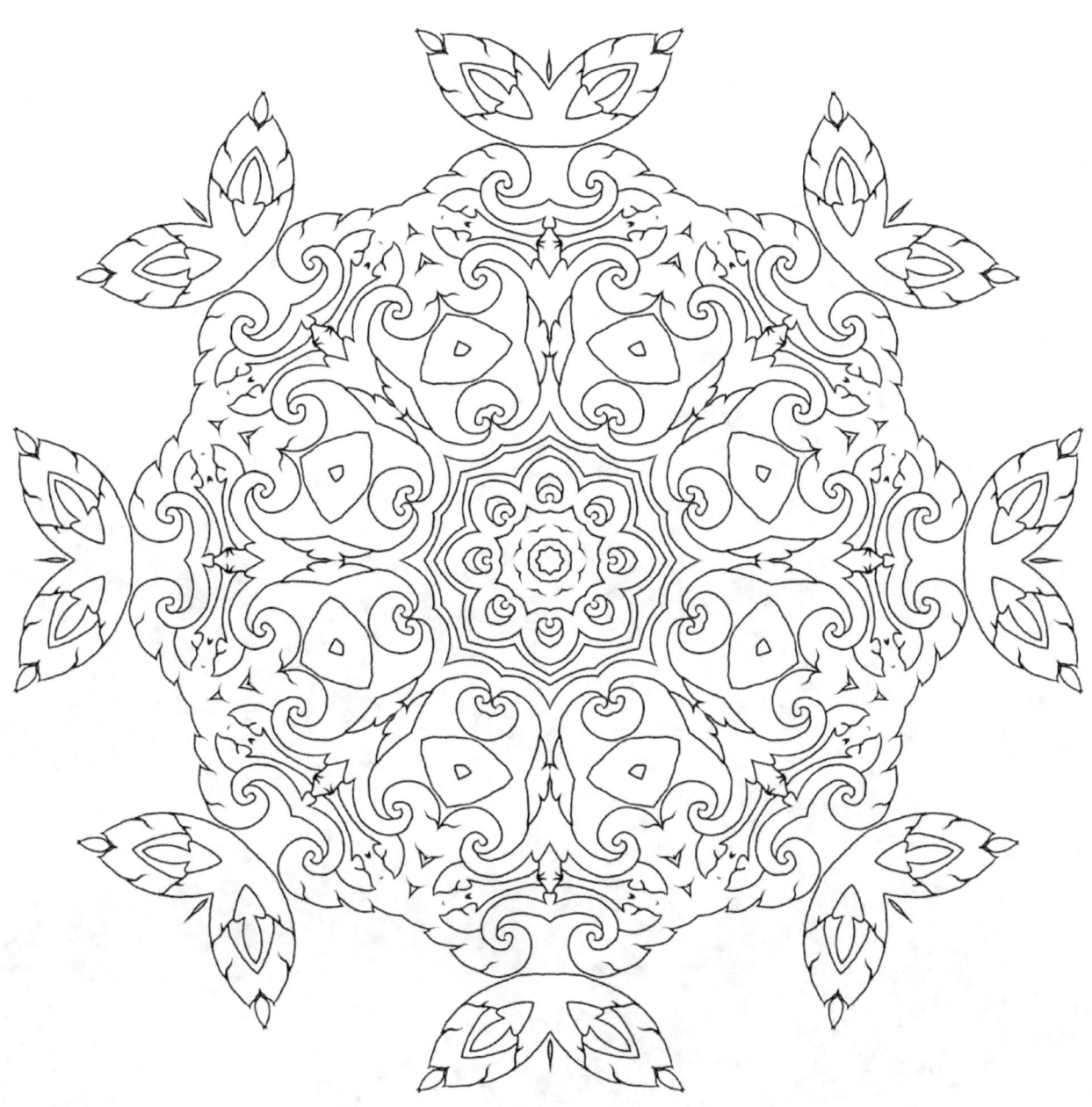

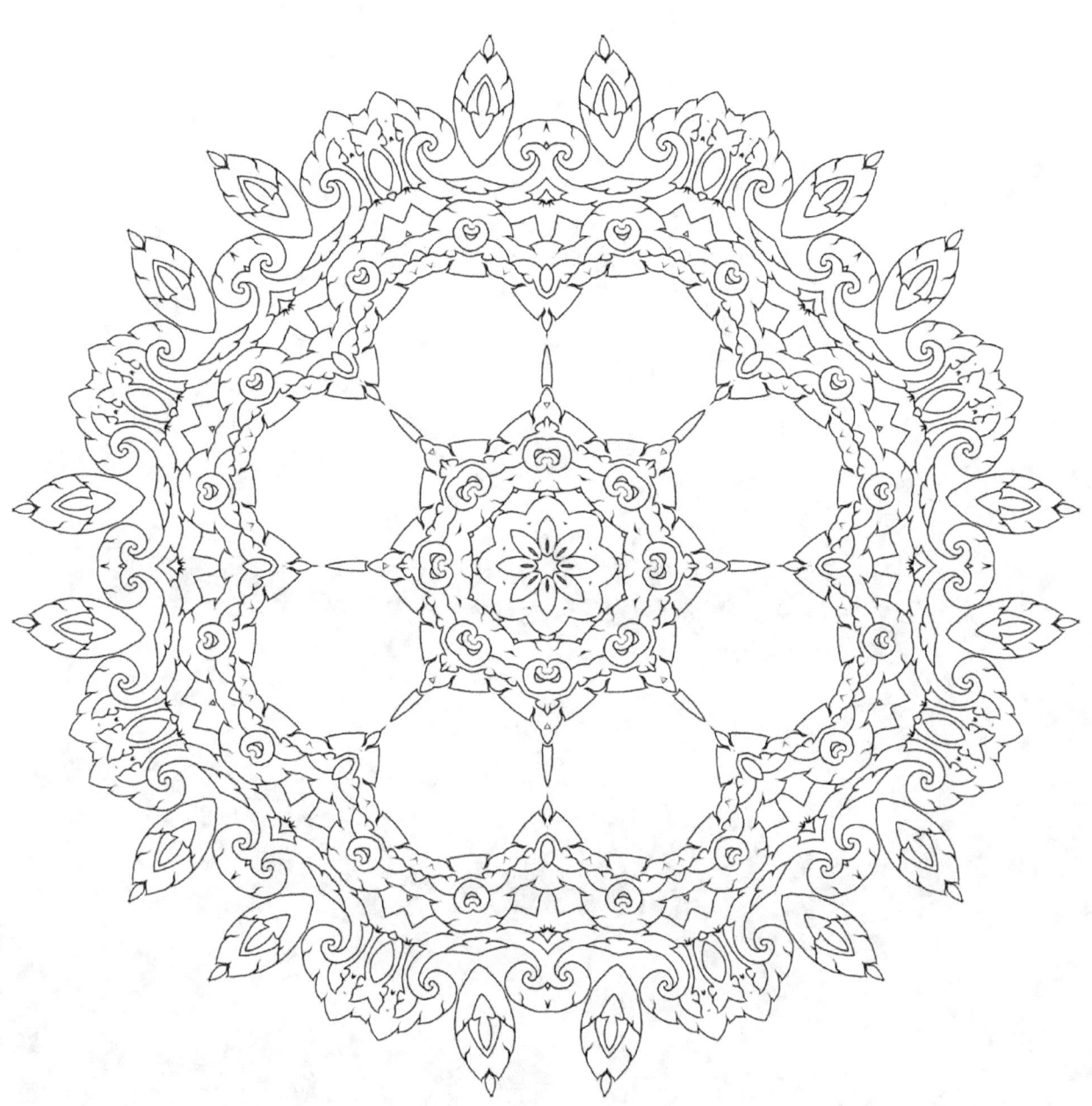

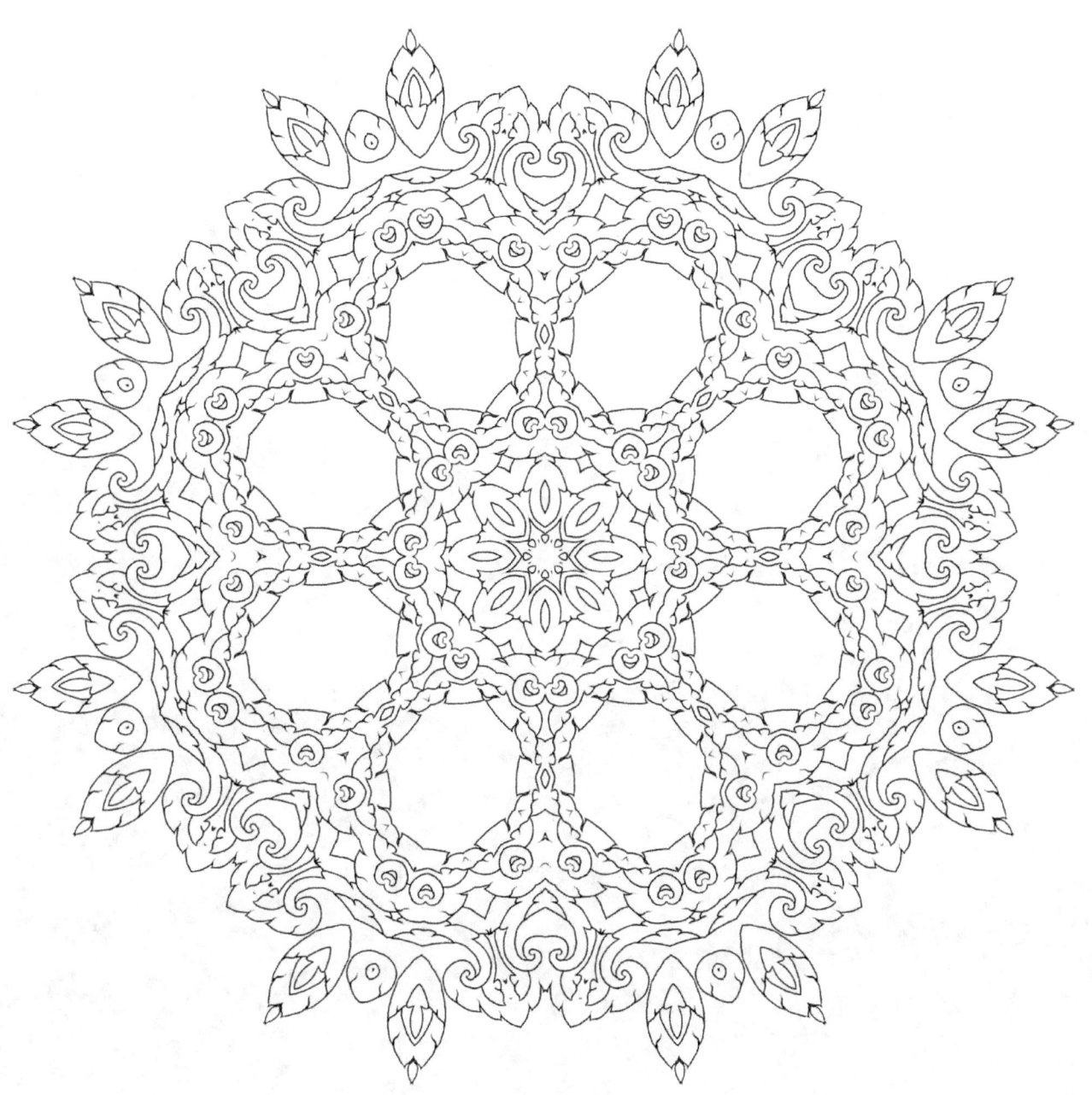

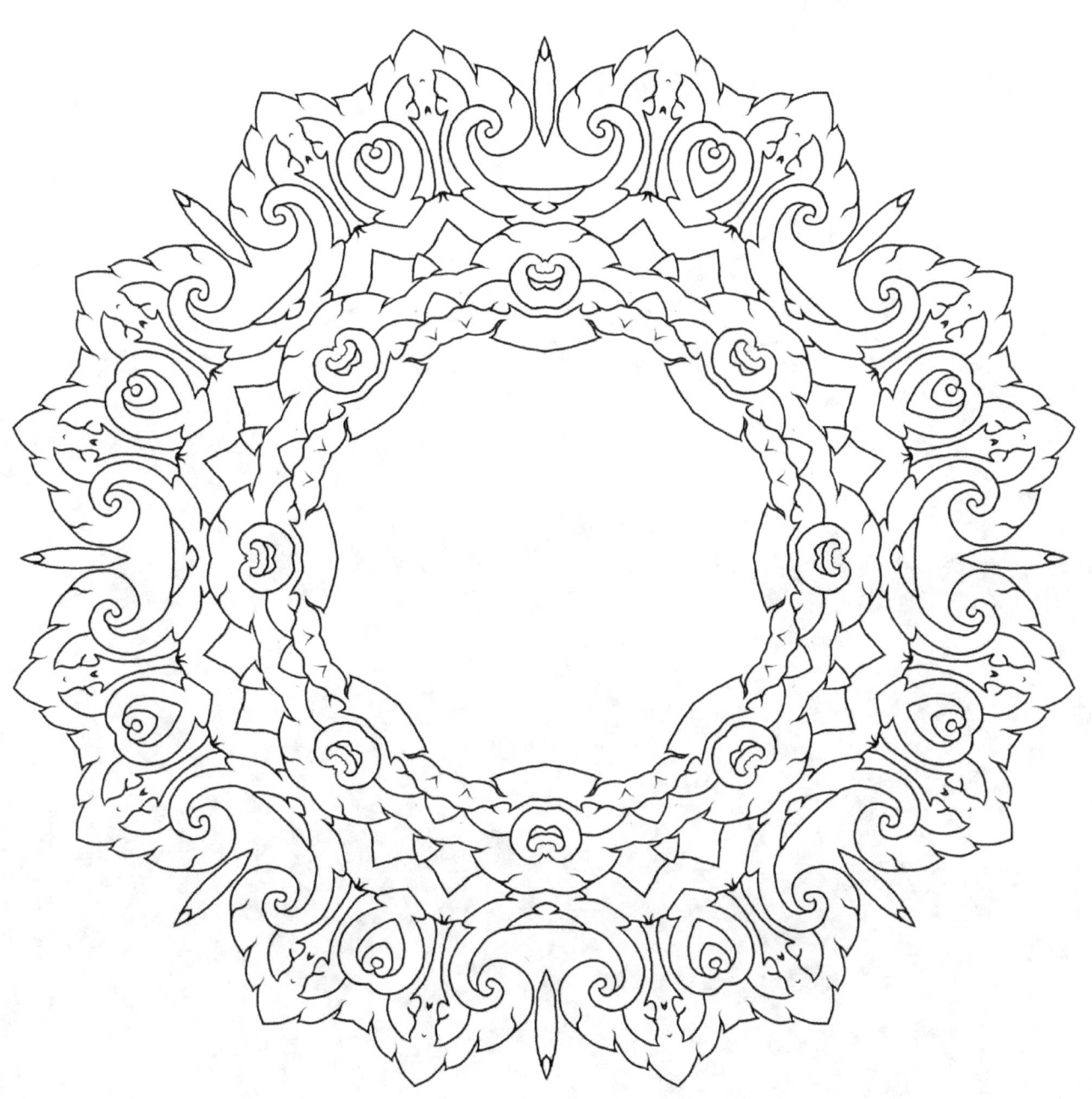

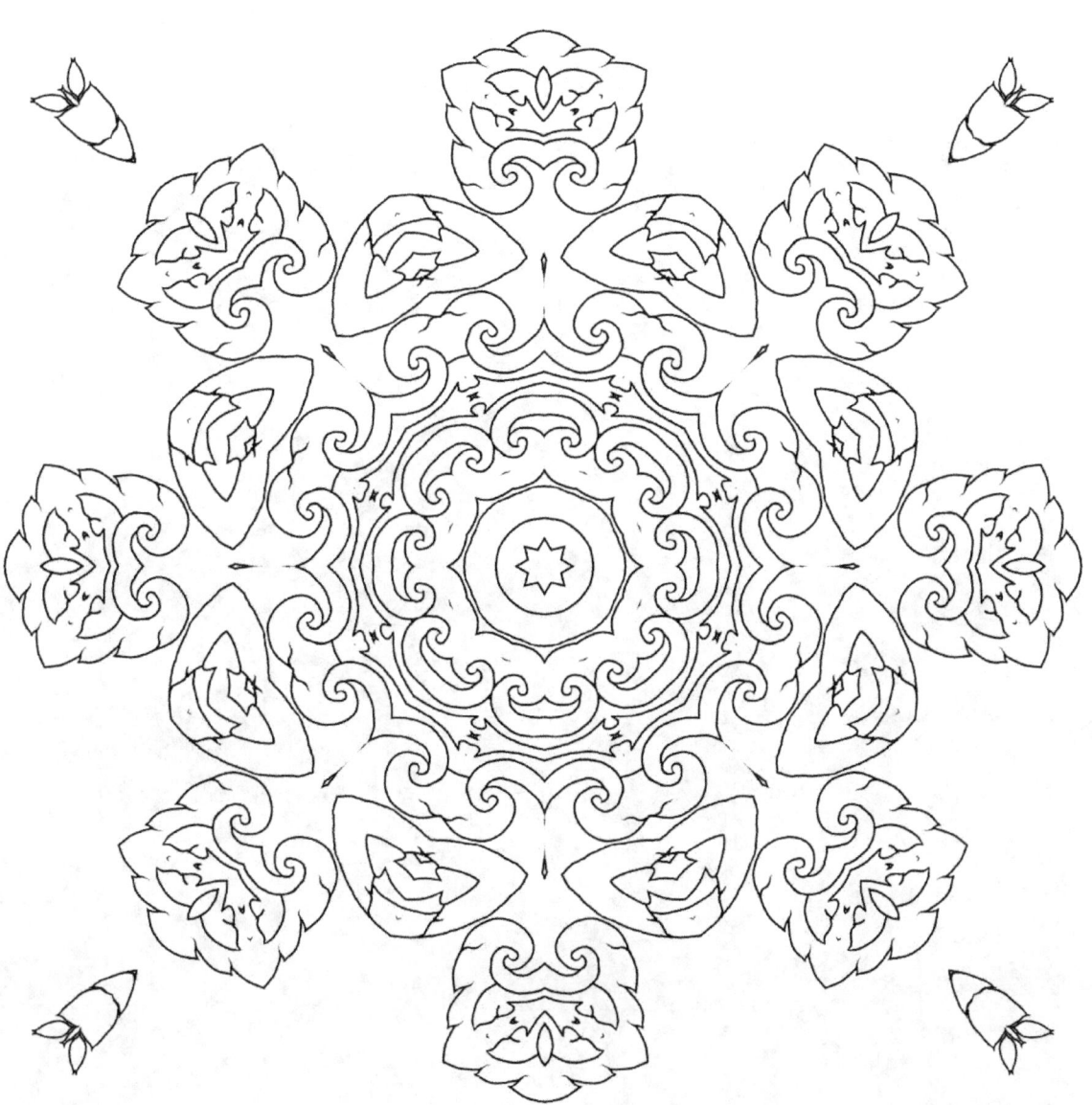

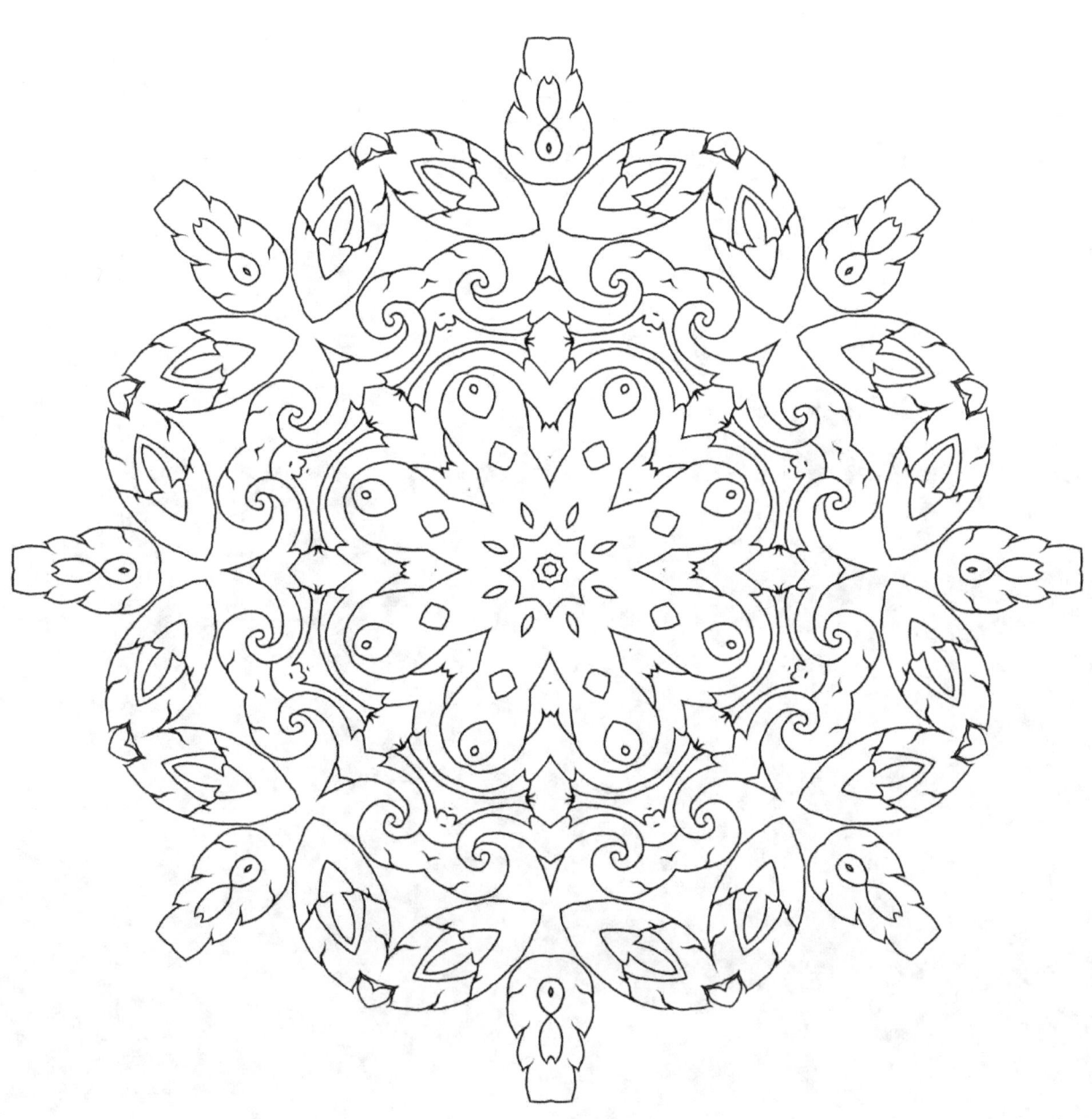

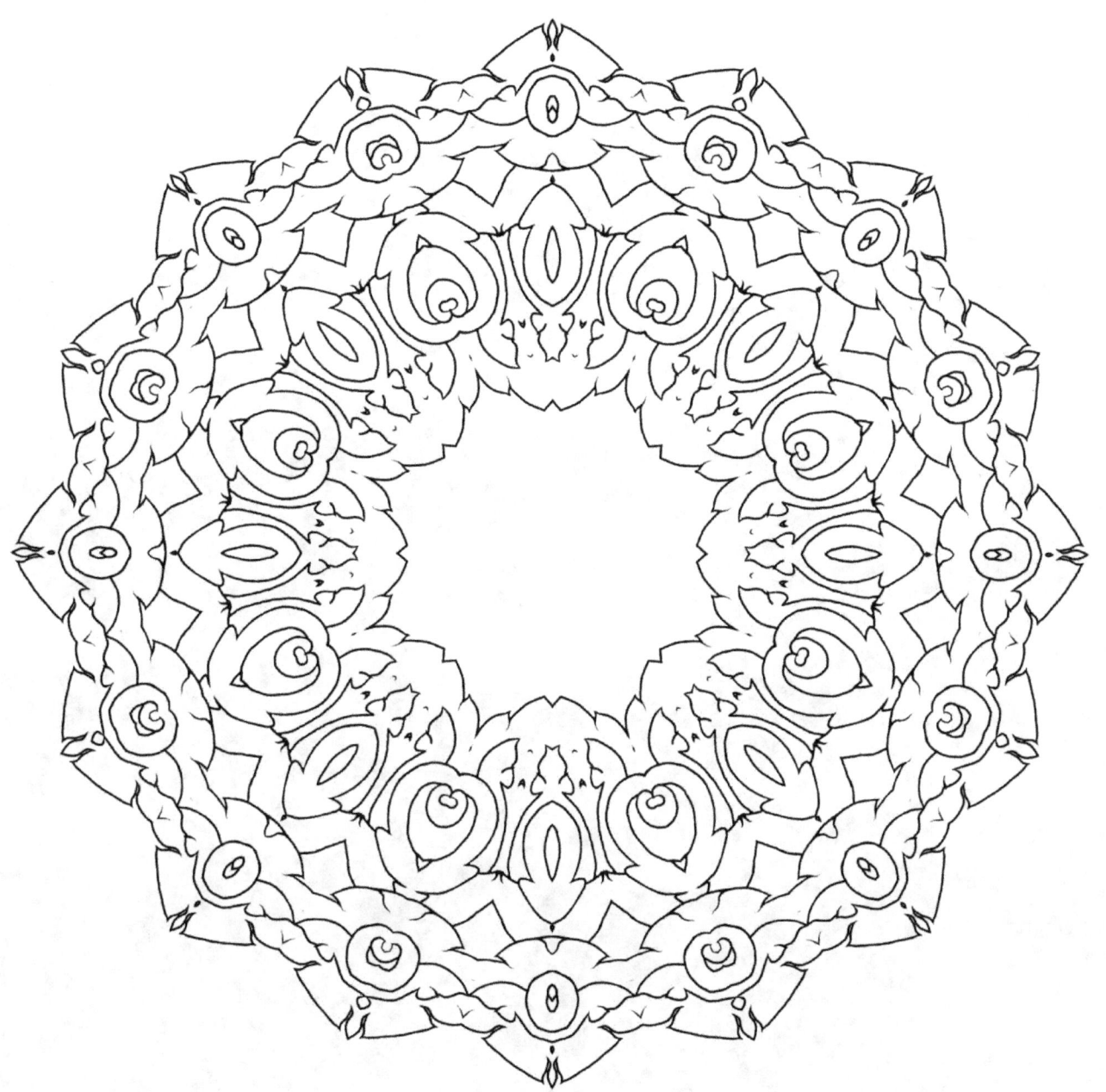

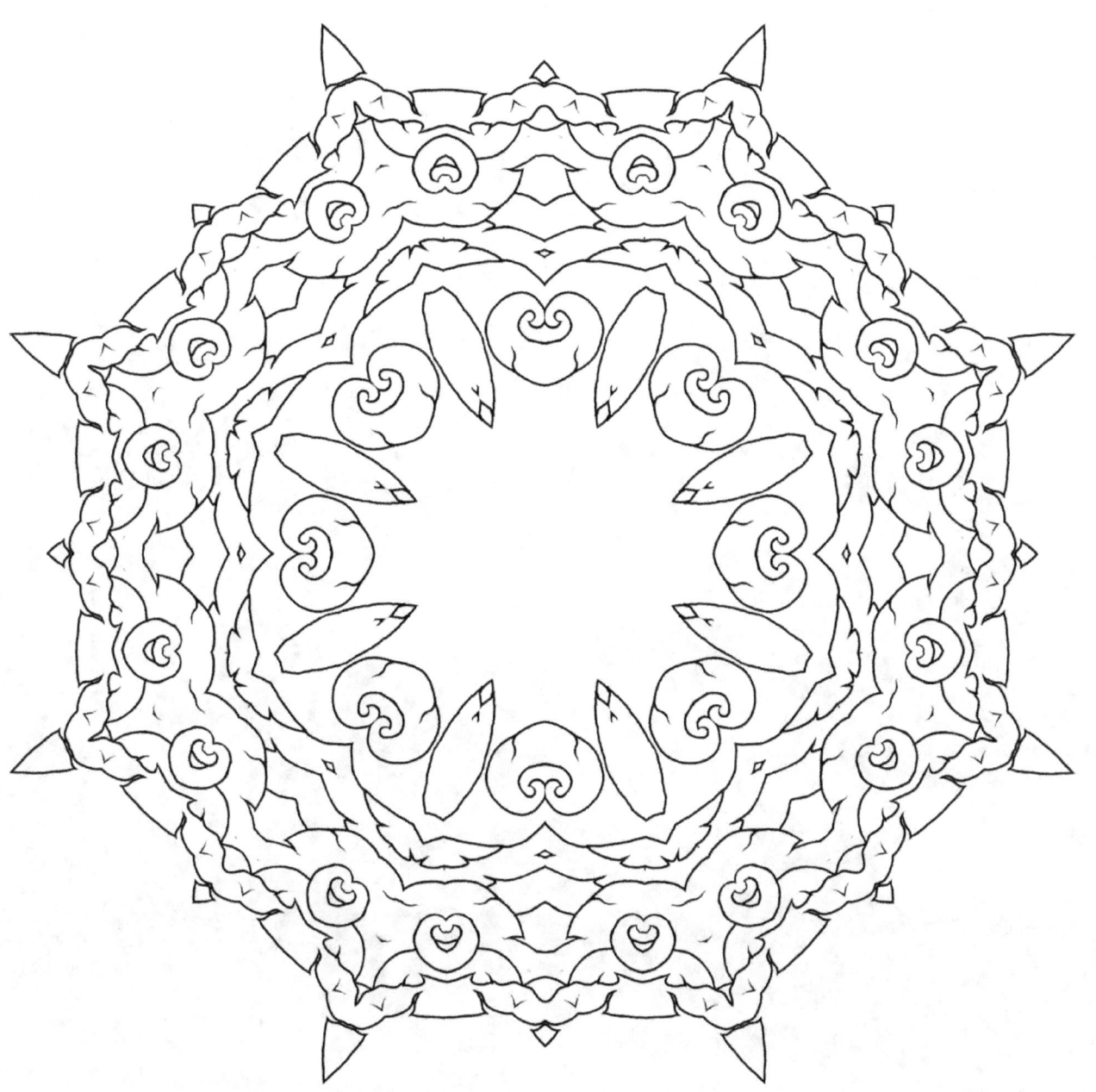

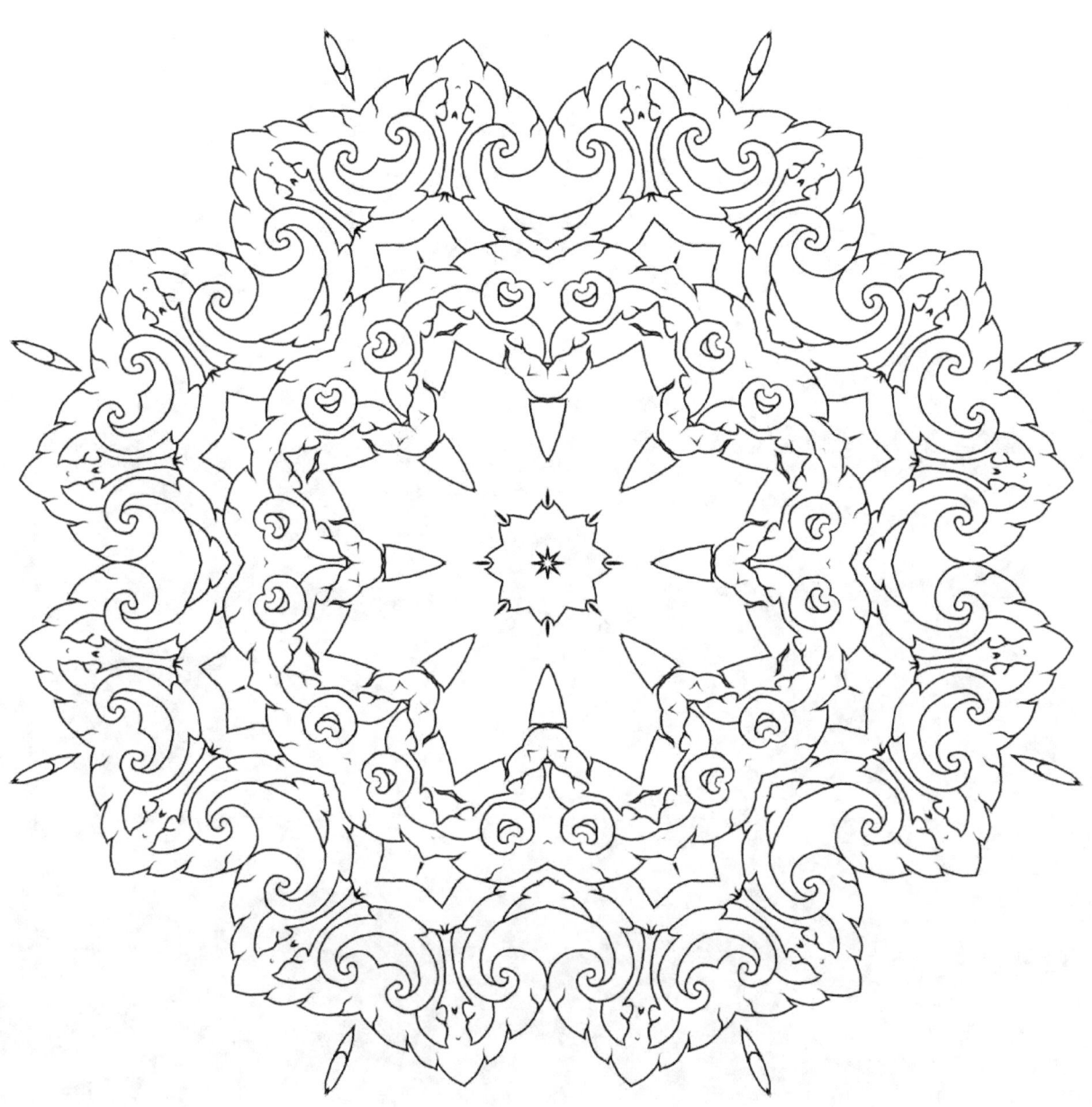

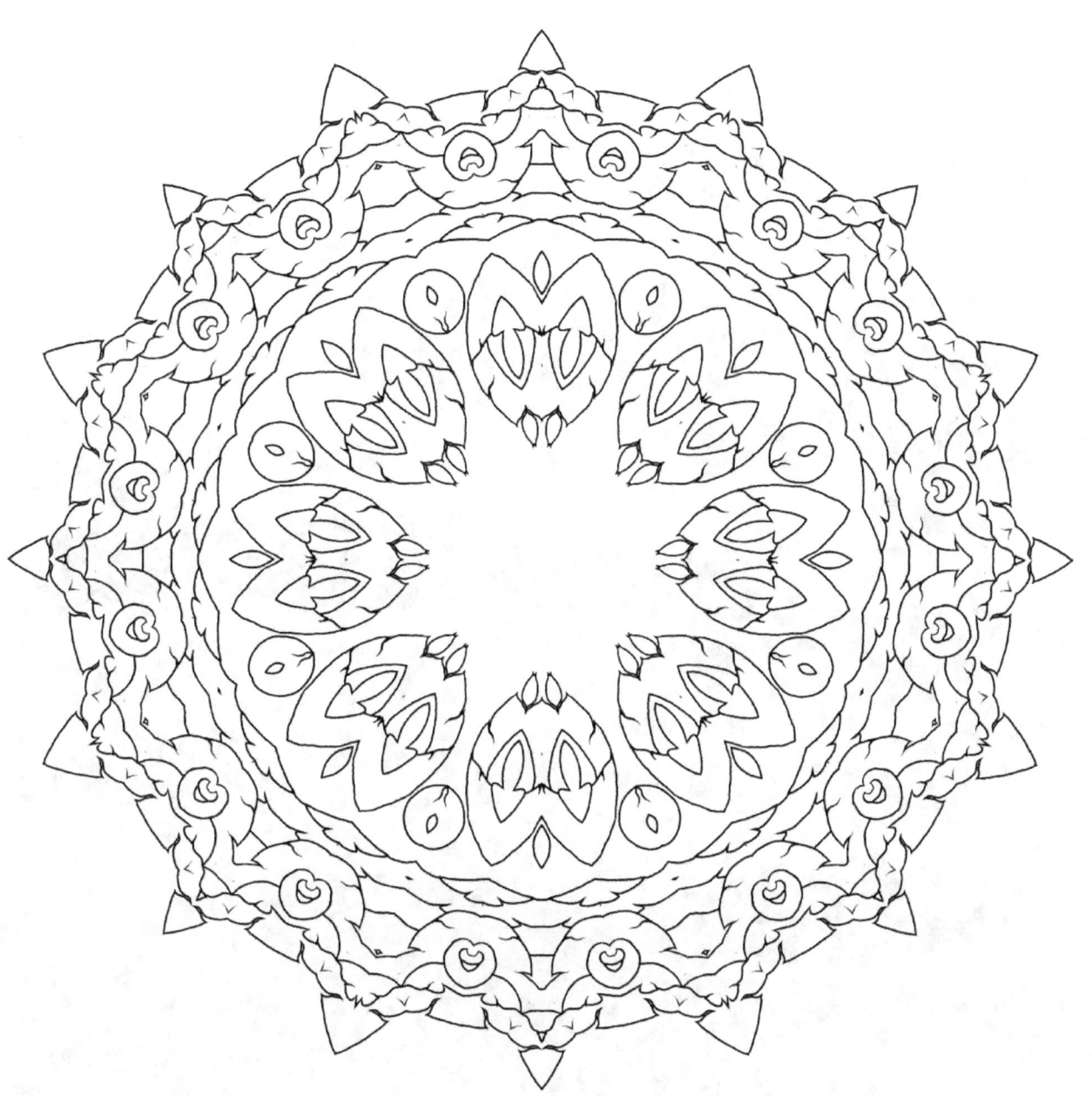

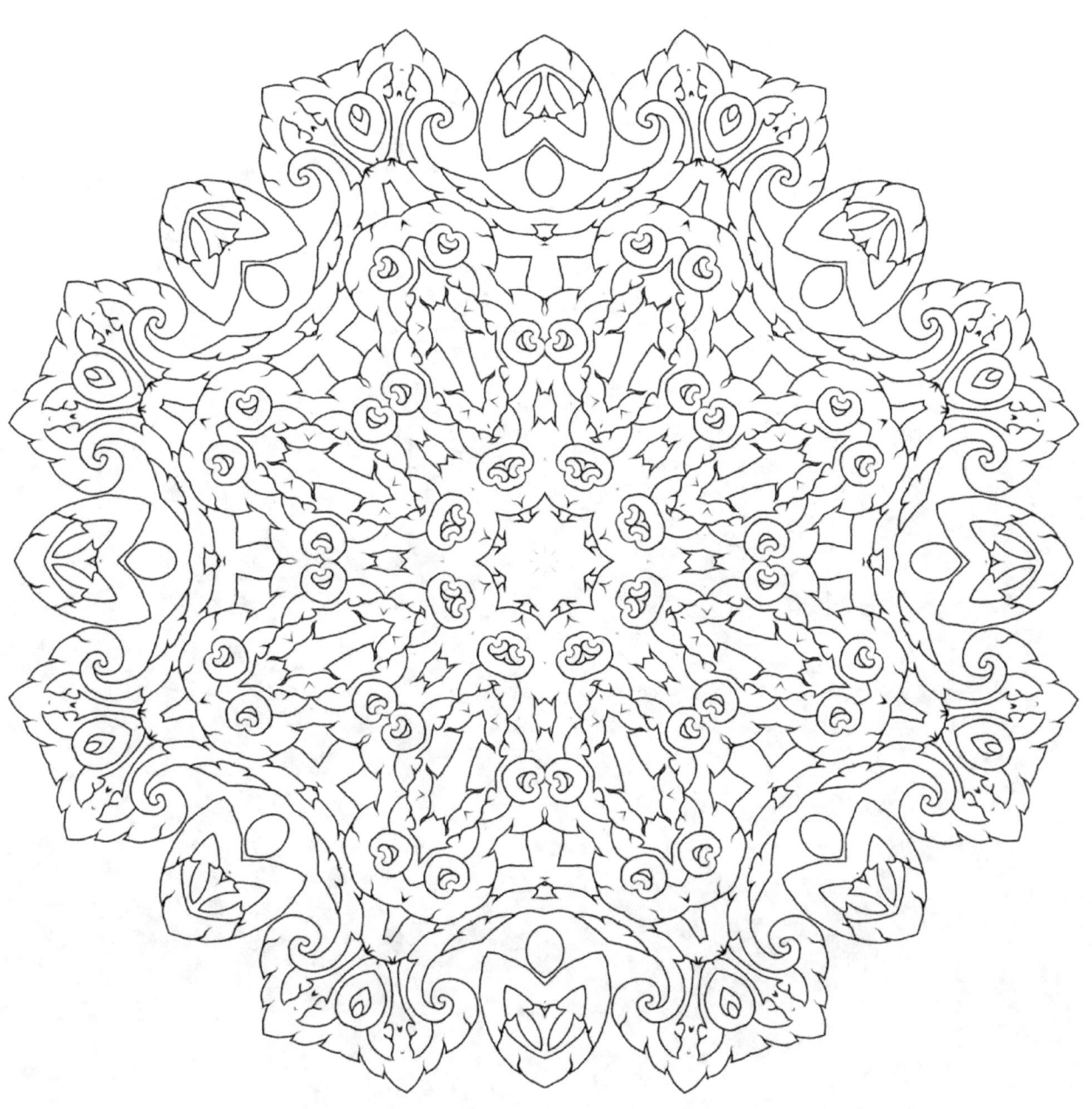

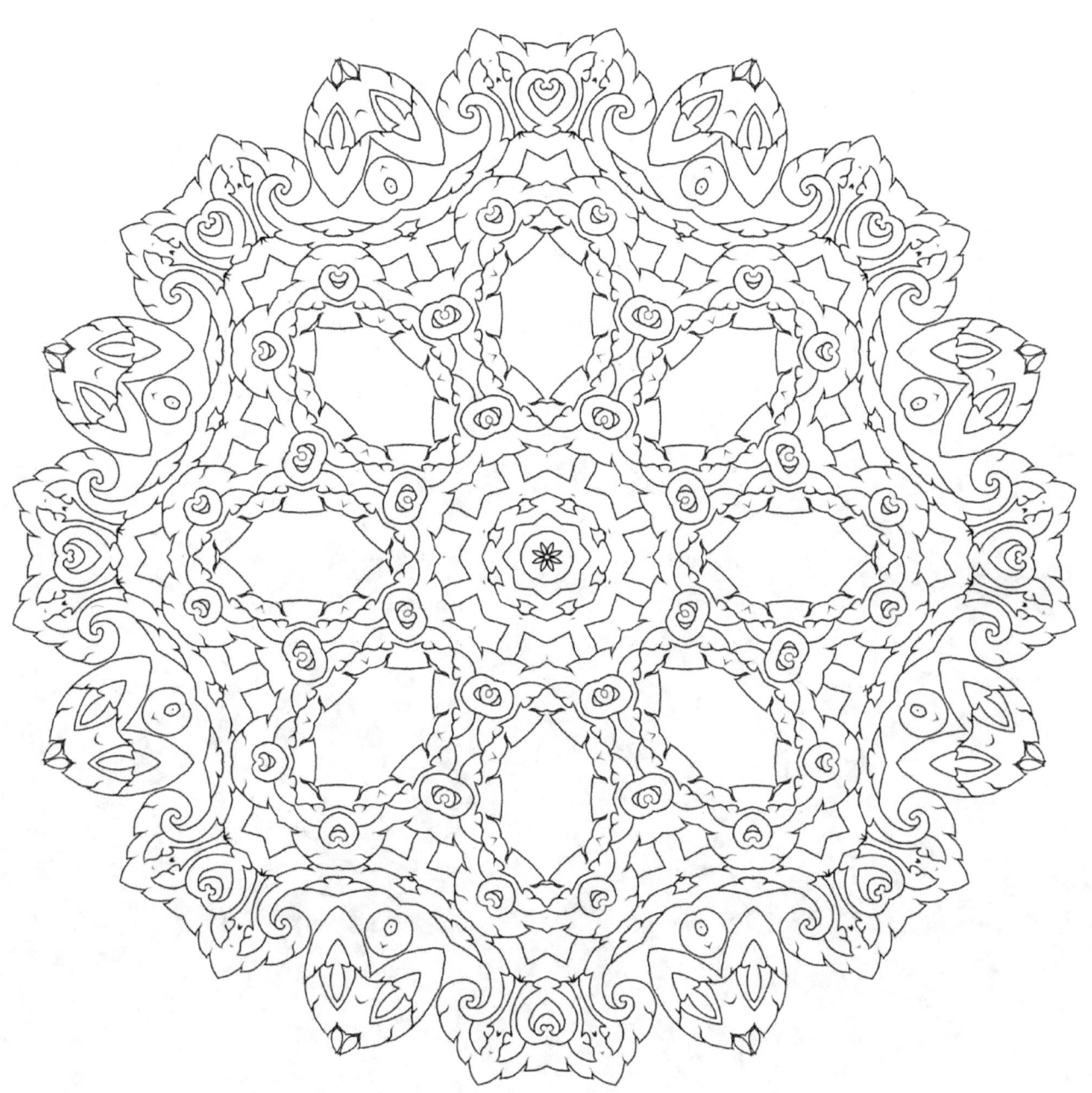

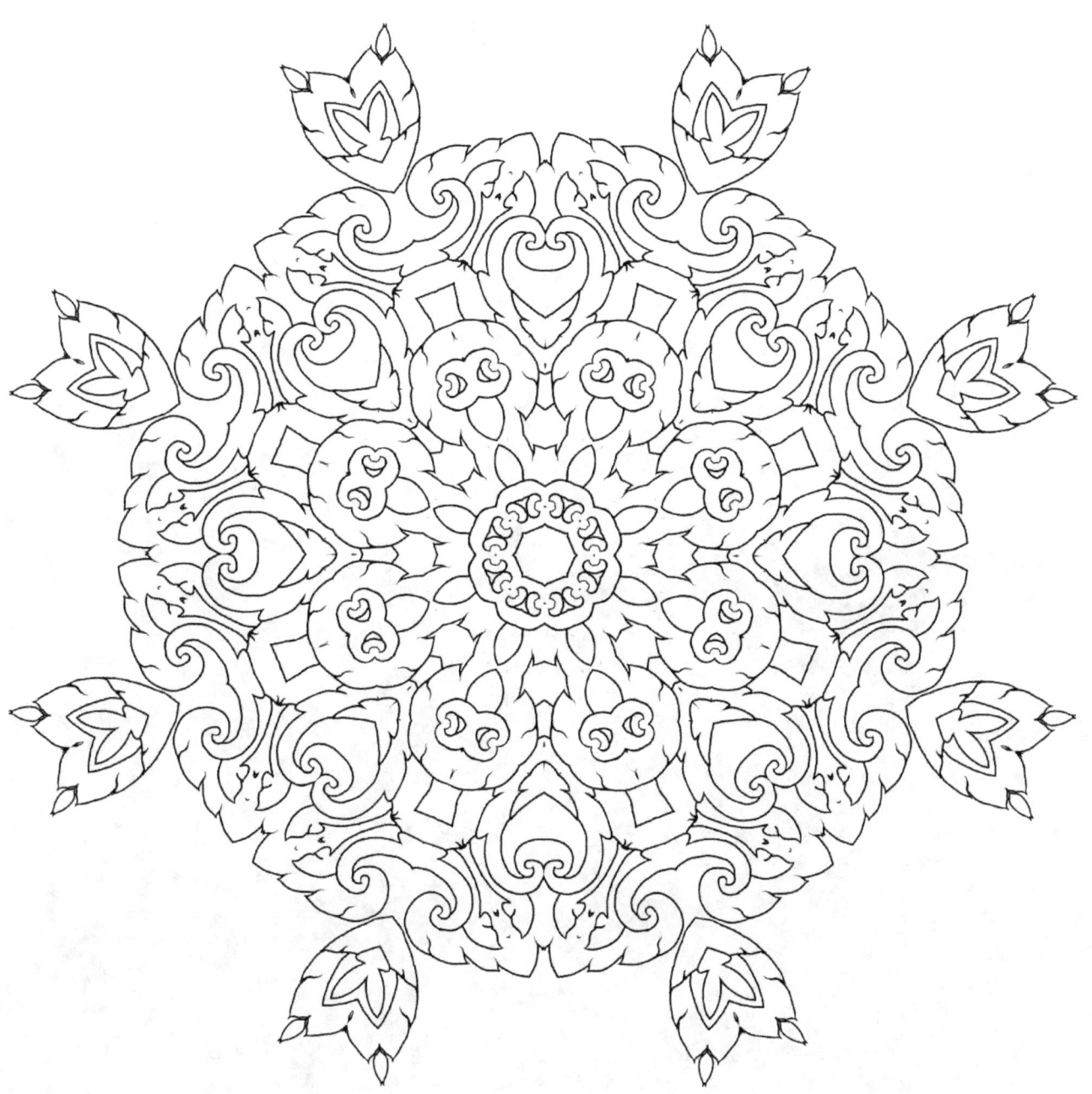

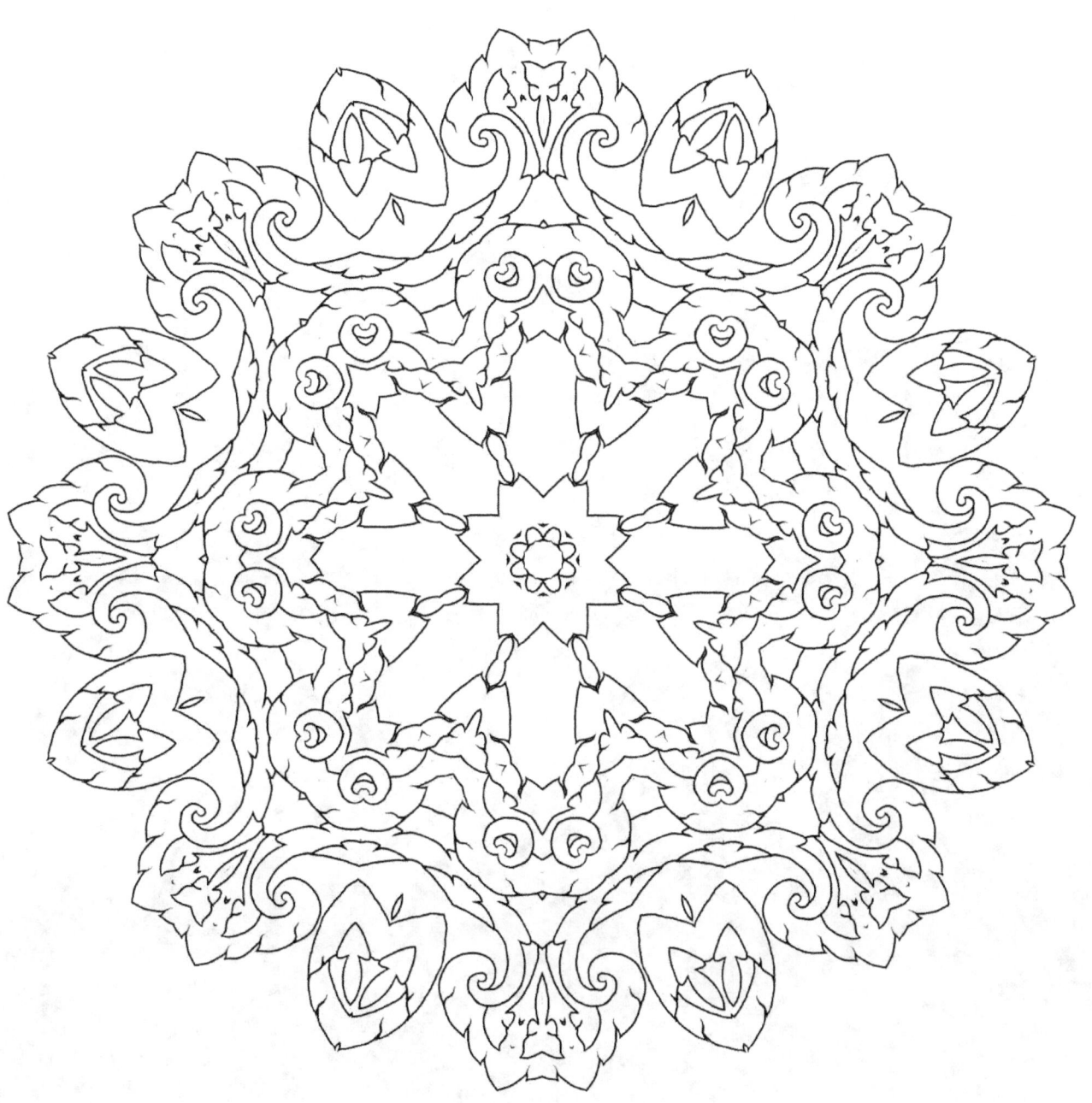

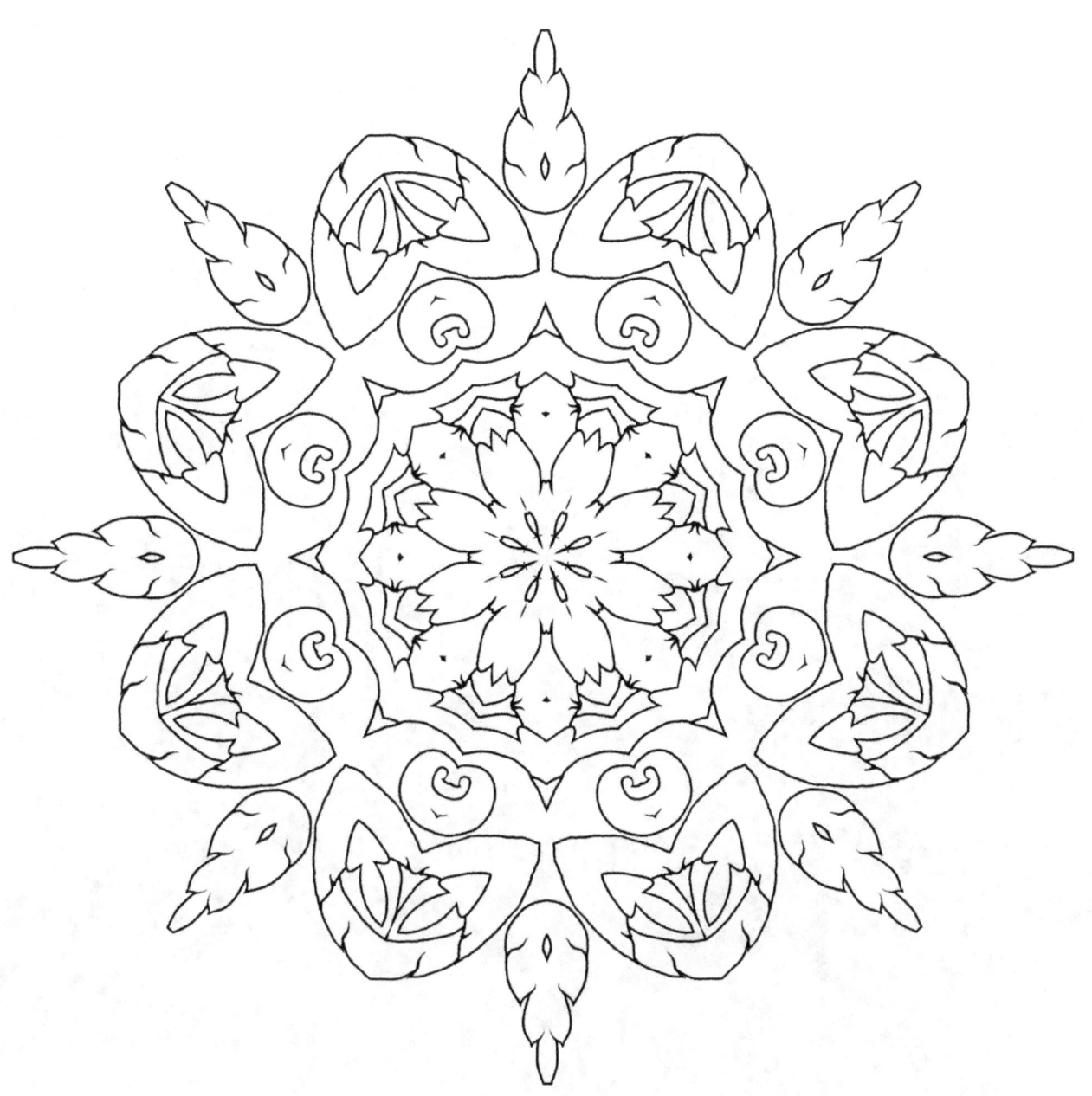

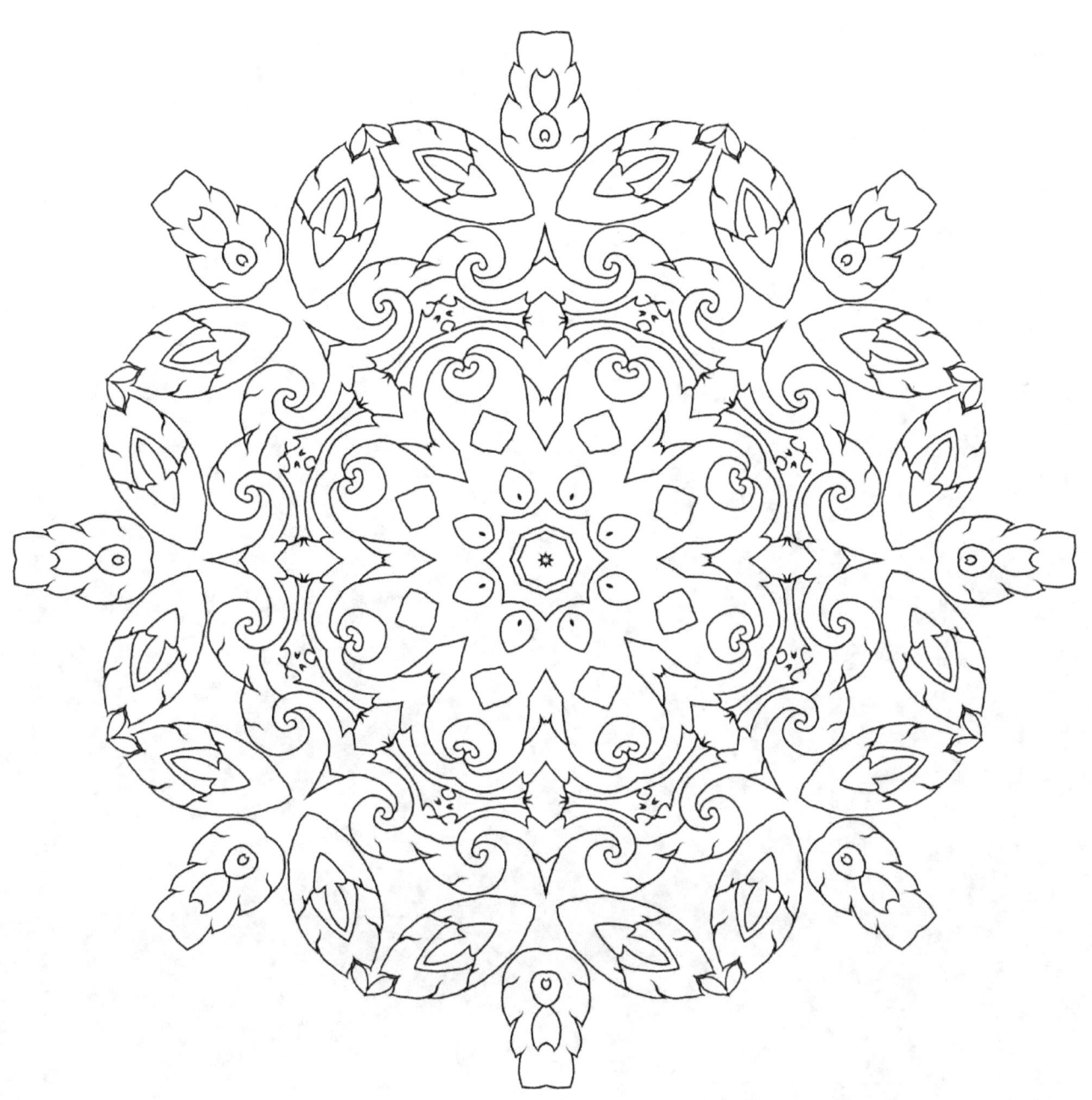

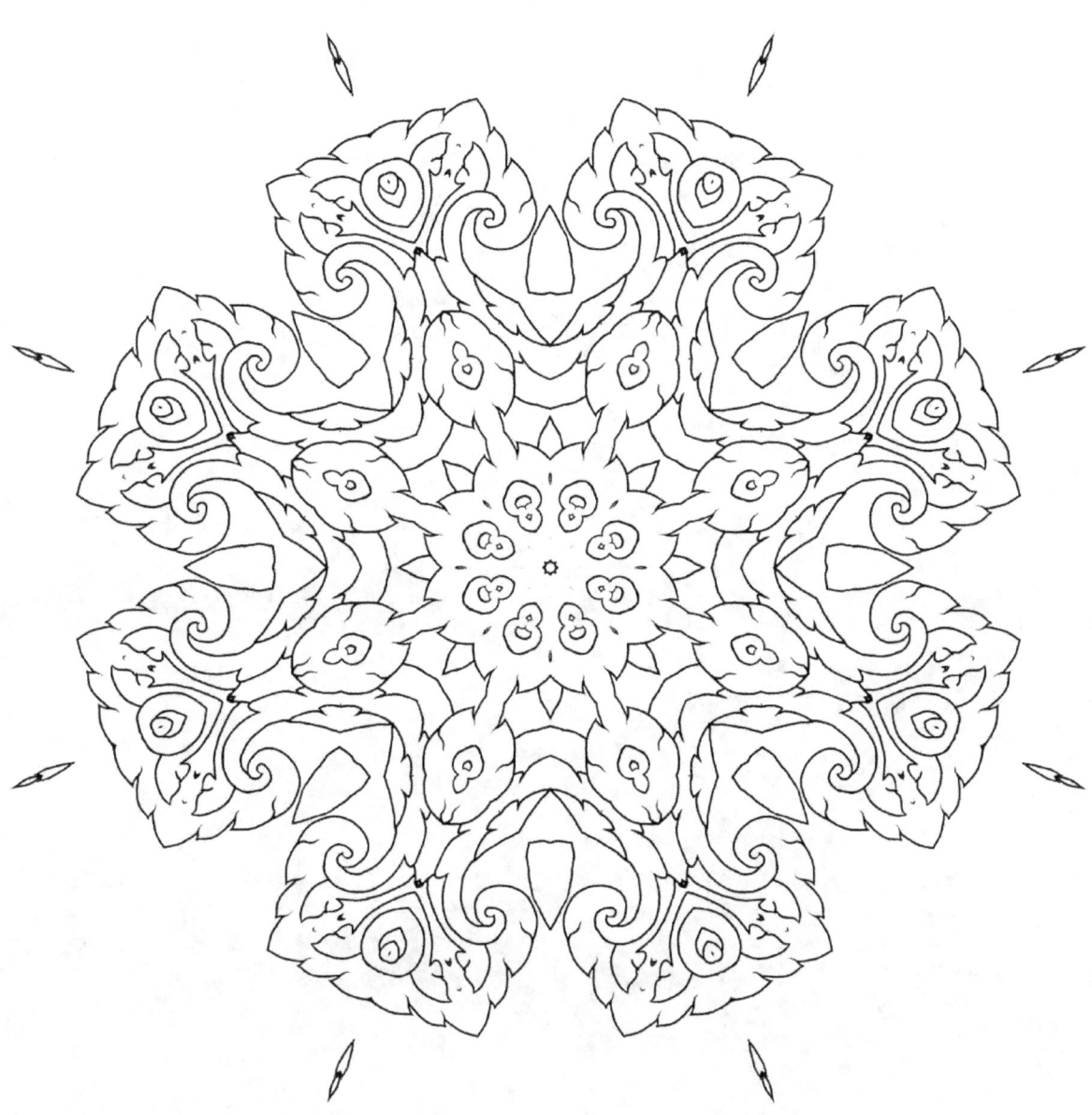

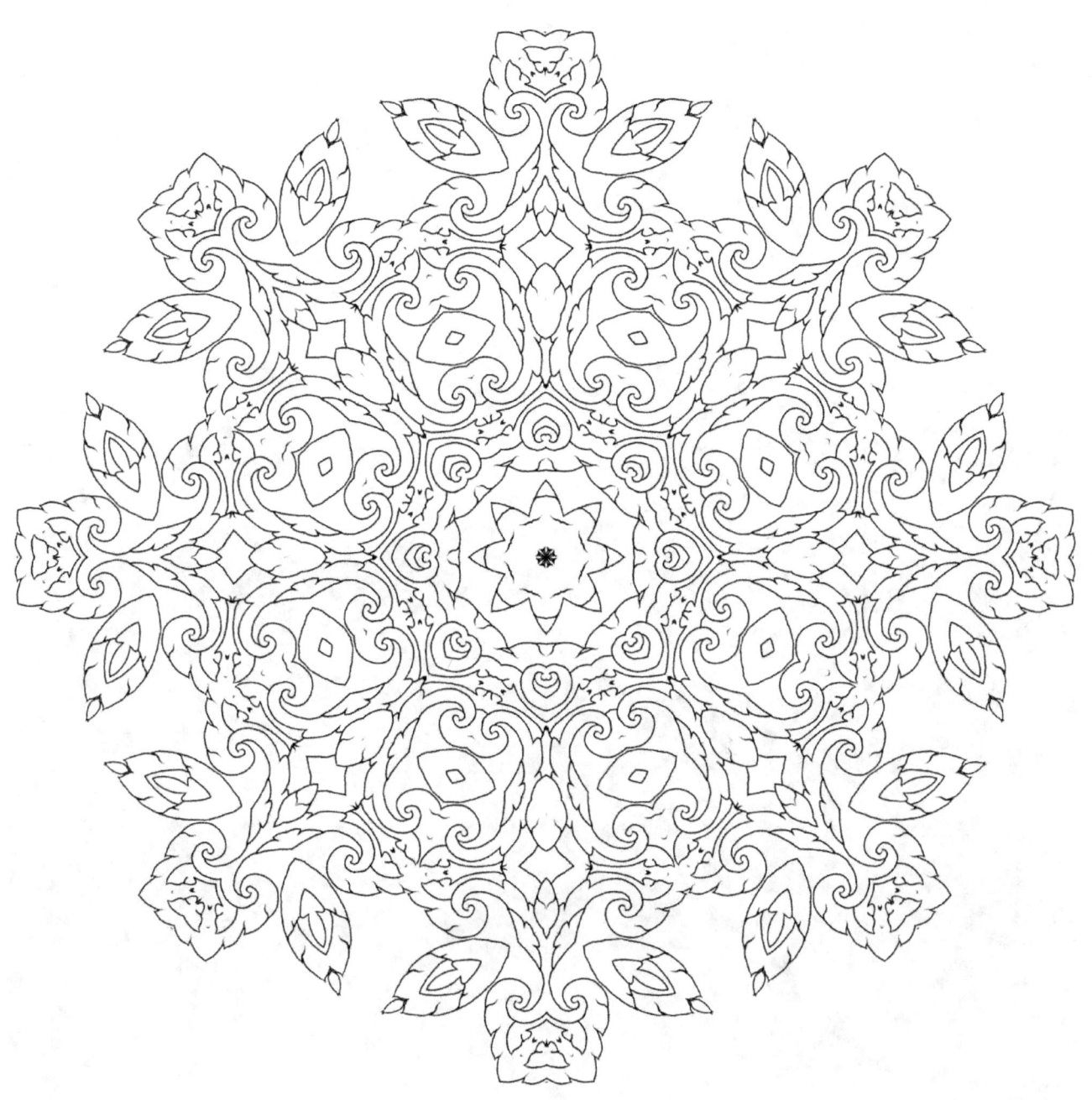

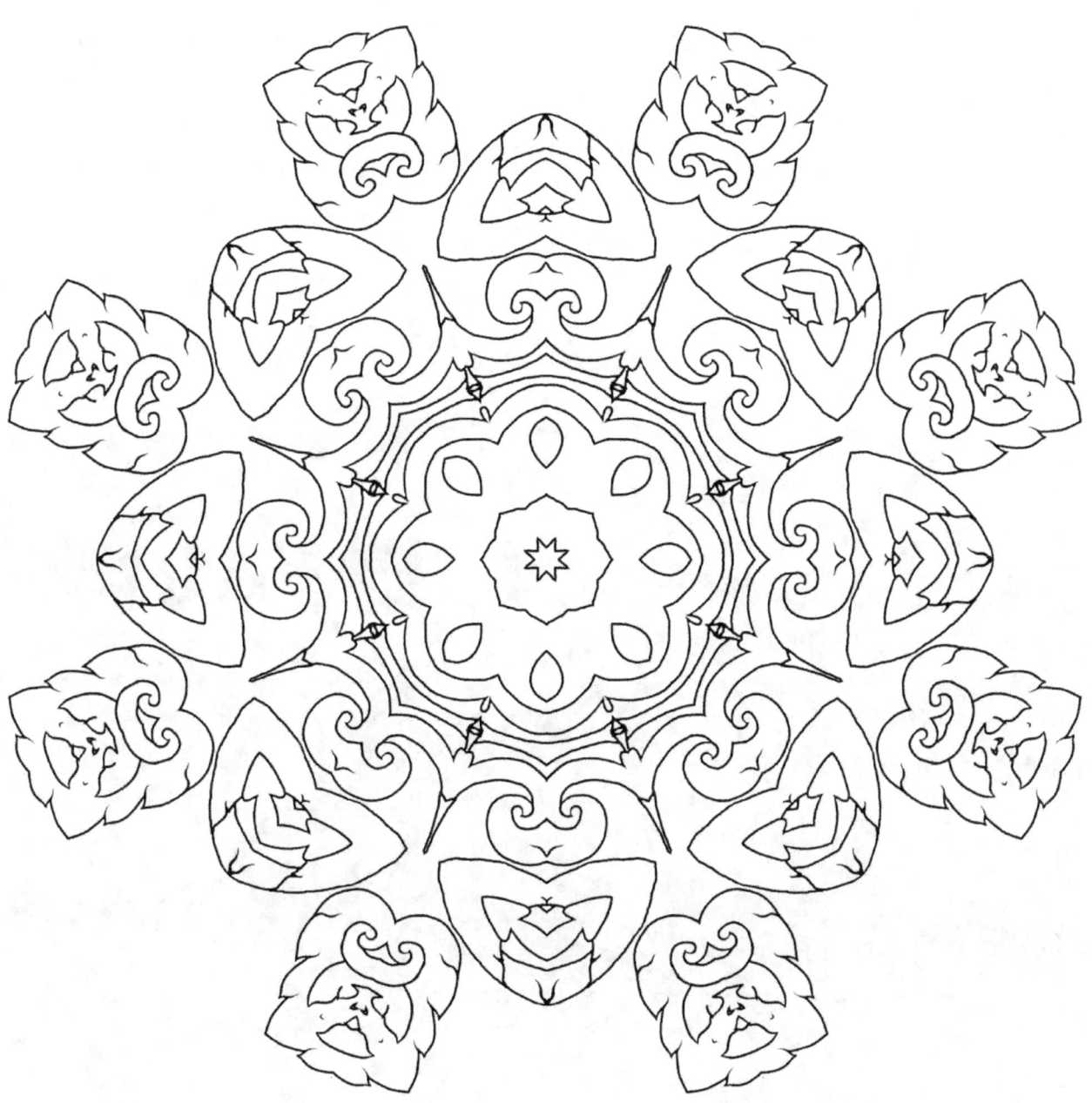

Thank you

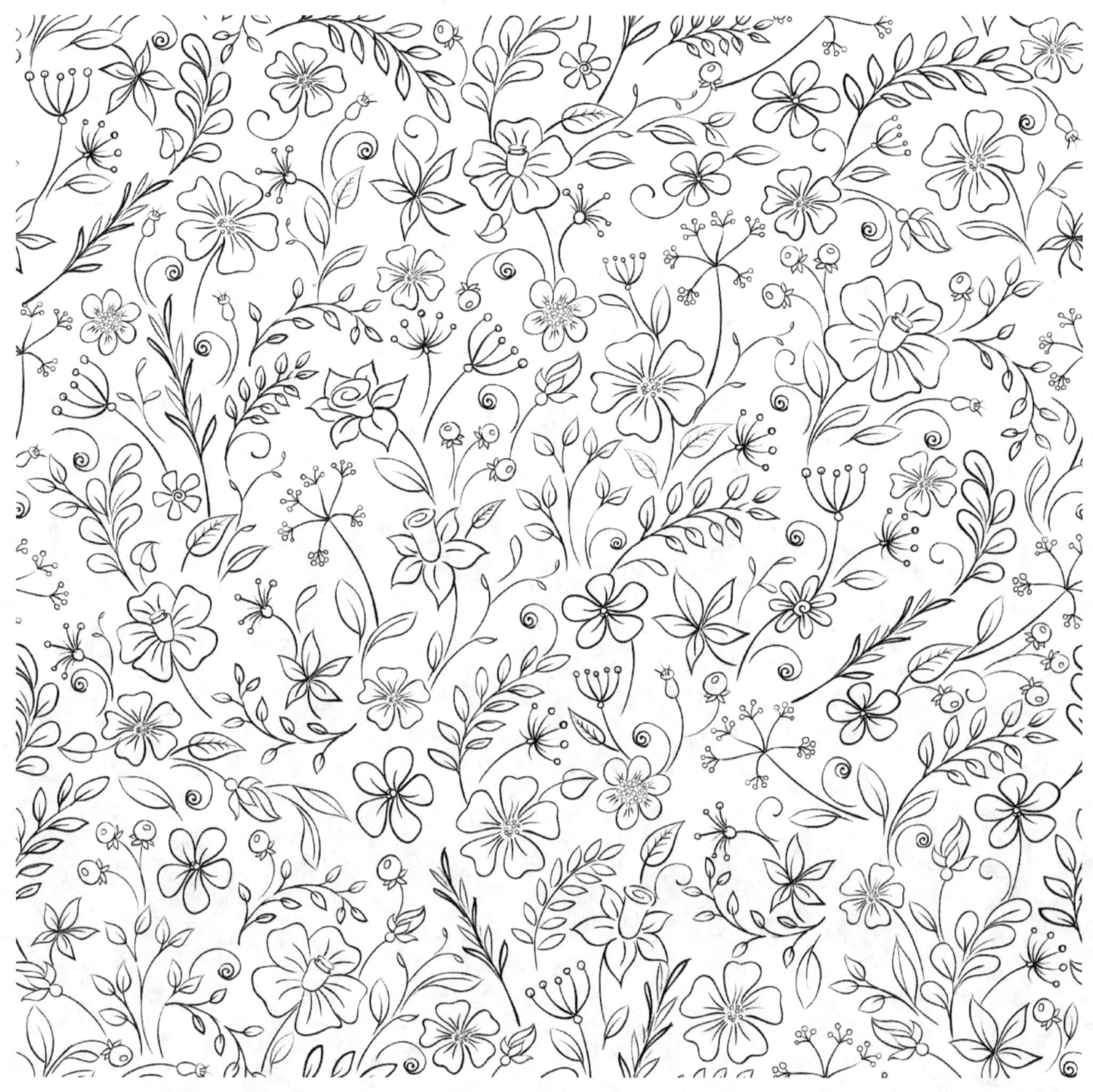

www.ingramcontent.com/pod-product-compliance
Lightning Source LLC
Chambersburg PA
CBHW081115180526
45170CB00008B/2850